Land of the Watchers

Land of the Watchers

Heather Lynn, Ph.D.

The
MIDNIGHT CRESCENT
PUBLISHING CO.
TRADEMARK

"The truth which I speak has been turned into a lie..."

— Sumerian tablet, excavated at Ur. ETCSL translation, c.5.2.4.

Published by The Midnight Crescent Publishing Company, Cleveland, Ohio, U.S.A.

ISBN-10: 1489598022
ISBN-13: 978-1489598028

For Tommy

ACKNOWLEDGEMENTS

This book is dedicated to my readers, especially: Heather Lynn Gregory, a strong survivor and watcher in her own right, and Zac Florence, a very patient and thoughtful soul. I wish to extend a heartfelt thank you to John and Sally Chewter, my surrogate uncle and aunt. I also wish to thank Ken Lemon, Hakan Ogun, Markus Jäckle, Peter Jacobson, Steve Asher, Jim Logue, Peter Jacobson, Dennis Mallon, Chris Petrillo, Ken Lipson, Laurie Welch, Chris Barger, Lisa Adler, Cindy Parker, Jenni Coe, Eduardo Romero, Alison Morris, Paul Myles, Amy Scott, Barbie Parker, Christine Hawk, Margaret Weston, R.J. Archer, Richard Lorenzo Roberts, Stuart Ahumada, Dashiell Cabasa, Fiorian Tichie, John Goessart, Josh Logan, Gary Edwards, Clifford Douglas Hawke, Christoph Sinnen, and everyone who has supported my work, and the mission of the Society for Truth in Archaeological research (S.T.A.R.).

A special thank you to the Fadernauts; an amazing group of enlightened free-thinkers, taking on the world one night at a time with Jimmy Church on Fade to Black.

CONTENTS

INTRODUCTION

It's been a few years since my report, *The Sumerian Controversy*, was published. Thanks to my readers, colleagues, and a few whistleblowers, I have learned that there is so much more to the story than I could have ever imagined. While some have criticized my tactics, I do not regret publishing my initial brief report when I did. Rather than confine myself to my pre-existing beliefs, specialized knowledge, and geographic region, I chose to publish what I knew and what I was still looking for, so that others could help through collaboration. Had I waited, I may have never had the opportunity to speak with so many people and learn how deep this all really goes.

The Sumerian Controversy is the first installment of my *Mysteries in Mesopotamia* series; a series which I consider an "open source" research project. This book, *Land of the Watchers*, is the second installment, a culmination of research, first-hand accounts, whistleblower testimony, and analysis. Some of the questions explored in the coming chapters ask: Why is the West in a continuous battle with the Middle East? Is it all really about oil? Why has gold been valuable in so many different cultures and civilizations throughout history? Is there lost technology beneath the desert sands? What were the real weapons of mass destruction? Why are the Sumerians so important to our understanding of human origins? Is there a parallel history that has been kept secret? Why have elite families been so obsessed with blood lineage and genetics?

I invite you to come with me down the rabbit hole one more time, as I try to uncover a secret that has been buried for nearly 4000 years; a secret that, if told, will change the lives of every living human on earth. Come with me, to the *Land of the Watchers*.

BACK TO MESOPOTAMIA

"The past slips from our grasp. It leaves us only scattered things. The bond that united them eludes us. Our imagination usually fills in the void by making use of preconceived theories... Archaeology, then, does not supply us with certitudes, but rather with vague hypotheses. And in the shade of these hypotheses some artists are content to dream, considering them less as scientific facts than as sources of inspiration."

—Igor Stravinsky

To recap just a bit, this all began in March of 2013, when I received an email from a gentleman claiming to have knowledge of a new discovery near the ancient Mesopotamian city of Ur. This was an amazing prospect, considering that the area has been off limits to researchers in light of the political climate in modern day Iraq. After confirming the story, I found that there indeed were new excavations underway in a little known place called Tell Khaiber.

What makes this site so special is that until recently archaeologists have avoided Ur and the surrounding sites for security reasons. Only a handful of groups like the Global Heritage Fund

(GHF), an NGO based in California, have traveled to the area. Over the past 30 years, the region has succumbed to wars and violence. As a result, Ur was officially closed to foreign archaeologists. After the 1950s revolution that toppled Iraq's monarchy, a nearby military air base was installed, making the site off limits to foreign archaeologists for sixty years.

With the U.S. invading in 2003 to remove Saddam Hussein from power, Baghdad's struggling government and economy were forced to deal with greater priorities than funding archaeological excavations. Iraqis had to focus on rebuilding their current cities, rather than rebuilding cities from their past.

Thus, the new excavations were both surprising and exciting. These were the first foreign excavations in southern Iraq since the 1930s, when a British and American team, led by Sir Charles Leonard Woolley, son of George Herbert Woolley, excavated Ur in the 1920s and the 1930s. Woolley's excavations resulted in some of the most important discoveries of modern time, a point we will examine further in the next chapter.

With the importance of Ur, and the understanding of how limited further research has been, it is easy to see why when satellite images showed the presence of a large temple-like structure in the area, researchers jumped at the opportunity. The excavation of the site officially broke ground in March, 2013 as a joint collaboration between British and Iraqi teams. A six-member British team worked with four Iraqis to dig in the southern province of Thi Qar, some 200 miles south of Baghdad, more than 10 miles from Ur. This site is the first major archaeological discovery so close to the city's center.

Three weeks of work at the site confirmed the presence of at least one monumental building. Satellite images showed it to be square, and to measure at least 250 square feet. There are rows of rooms encircling a grand courtyard. The rooms excavated along the eastern side of the building have solid pavements of regular mud bricks. The walls are nine feet thick, indicating that whatever was behind these walls was of immense importance. One large hall has a series of beautifully decorated floors further pointing to this being a sacred site.

Such a monumental complex is an uncommon discovery. It is extremely unusual to find complexes this old at such a massive scale. Early theories were that it was a temple, palace, or "administrative center," dating back at least 4,000 years.

The structure isn't the only interesting discovery at the site. Some of the early artifacts reported were a 3½ inch clay plaque, depicting a worshiper dressed in a long fringed robe, and assorted pottery fragments. Fragments of vessels made from stone, including a piece of ivory have also been excavated, various tools made of copper and stone, a rim fragment from a once magnificent alabaster bowl, and not one, but two molded clay plaques showing a male worshipper and a female figure, respectively. Also found was the shallow grave of an infant, buried just under the surface. Its body had been placed into a pottery jar which was then laid on its side.

Tablets were also found, some just lying right on the surface of the ground. This is astonishing since they are made of unbaked clay, making them very fragile. The tablets were sent for analysis but early clues as to what they said were a partial list of men's names, along with their father's names, which indicates a record patriarchal lineage, and possibly, elite bloodlines. The names were apparently Babylonian in origin. A small piece of a tablet makes mention of orchards and gardens, like those in the Garden of Eden. Another tablet fragment referenced the city's governor, leading us to theorize that the settlement at Tell Khaiber was at least significant enough to have a governor. The administrative center idea has emerged as the leading theory.

In addition to pottery, tablets, and bodies, a mysterious item made from rare and expensive diorite was found, baffling archaeologists. Diorite is a gray rock that is relatively rare and extremely hard, making it notoriously difficult to work with. It is so hard that ancient civilizations used diorite balls to work granite. The use of diorite in art was important in Mesopotamian empires as well as both the Inca and Mayan civilizations. The Inca and Mayan civilizations used diorite in their fortress walls and weaponry; a testament to its strength. Theories for what this artifact is have ranged from a recycled chip from a larger relic, to a game piece. No one knows for sure.

After excavating some of the site, the archaeologists used a gradiometer to measure the site's magnetic field. A gradiometer is a special type of magnetometer with multiple sensors: one closer to the ground to collect magnetic data about the surface, and the other located above the first sensor to collect information about the Earth's magnetic field. An archaeologist would then subtract one reading from the other, essentially filtering out the noise from the Earth's magnetic field, allowing subtle features of archaeological interest to be detected.

In theory, the gradiometer could record magnetic differences between the walls and rooms of the complex without disturbing the deposits underneath. This way, they could locate any other possible buildings. As of 2013, the site's magnetic field is actively being researched and recorded.

All of these interesting discoveries were published in a few standard press releases. Once learning the details, I immediately contacted the university involved for questions. After initially being granted an interview, I was given the cold shoulder and was unable to maintain meaningful contact moving forward. As a result, I decided to investigate the financial supporters of this excavation (follow the money).

This led me to discover a tangled web of big oil, global banks, elite industrialist families, secret societies, U.S. presidents, and Nazis. Yes, Nazis. If you have not already, you can read more about my experience in *The Sumerian Controversy*. I will be going into greater detail about this later but first, here are the latest developments.

Latest Developments: 2013

Once the initial excavation wrapped up, an official report was issued by project backers by the British research team. The report included more details about what was found in 2013, including a diverse variety of tools, such as large grindstones, spindles, flint sickle fragments, pounders and grinders made from imported stone, and copper weapons. This shows that numerous economic activities took place in this administrative center, leading to great wealth.

Perhaps one of the more interesting discoveries, is that of a statue depicting the Mesopotamian goddess of healing, Gula, also known as Ninkarrak. Could this mean that the administrative center is actually a *healing* center? Before we can begin to answer this question, it is important for us to first look at who the goddess Ninkarrak was, and why is she so important.

Like most ancient gods, Ninkarrak was known by many different names through different periods of rulership; Gula, Ninisinna, Bau or Baba. Much later, she would be syncretized, or amalgamated based on religion, with Ishtar. In addition to having many different names, Ninkarrak had different titles including, "The Lady Who Makes the Broken up Whole Again," "The Great

Healer of the Black-headed Ones," "Herb Grower," and "Creates Life in the Land." All these titles are indicative of a vegetation goddess with regenerative power. In fact, she is credited as having "breathed life" back into mankind after the Great Flood. Ninkarrak did not only represent healing, gardens, and life creation, she also represented gateways. As the protector of boundaries, her image was frequently depicted on *kudurrus*, or boundary stones, like the one in Fig. 1-B.

Fig. 1-A: Bust of Ninkarrak: Limestone, (2150-2100 BCE). From Telloh, ancient Girsu, Louvre.

Fig. 1-B: The Kudurru of Gula, for the goddess Gula/Ninkarrak. (14th century or 13th century BCE). *Louvre.*

The Kudurru of Gula shows Gula/Ninkarrak seated on her chair with an adjacent dog, symbols of the gods, and cuneiform text.

12

Ninkarrak is the daughter of Anu and wife of the warrior god Pabilsag (in Isin), Ninurta (in Nippur) and Ningirsu (in Lagaš), and mother of three other healing deities: Damu, Ninazu and Gunurra. This revered healing goddess had many cult centers, including Nippur, Umma, Lagaš, Larsa, Uruk, Borsippa, Babylon, and Assur, but the most prominent cult center was Isin, where her temple was as named "Dog Temple."

In her temple in Isin, there were over 30 dog burials discovered, as well as many dog figurines. Although different theories abound, archeologists are still unsure as to why she is associated with the dog. My personal thoughts on this is that it somehow relates to the star Sirius, also known as "The Dog Star." I think the answer can be found in archaeoastronomy and Babylonian astrology.

Considering how Ninkarrak would eventually be seen as Ishtar (who would later be associated with Isis by the Egyptians), a comparative analysis of their iconography yields interesting connections. Firstly, Ishtar's main icons are the lion and the bull, or the constellations Leo and Taurus. In Babylonian creation myths, the constellation Leo was not known as a feline, but rather "The Big Dog." Just as gods were syncretized, often so were zodiacal symbols.

Moreover, ancient Sumerian texts sometimes refer to the lion as "Mul Ur-Gu-la" (Gula, the goddess, also means 'great') which translated means a great carnivore. This term is broad and has been used interchangeably to mean lion, dog, wolf, etc. Lastly, the bright star in Leo's chest was known by the Babylonians as "Regulus," meaning royal star. It was believed the elites born under this star would have victory and ultimate power over the people on Earth.

Every year there is an important alignment of Sirius and Leo, leading some to consider this a time of spiritual healing wherein souls are "initiated" into higher realms of consciousness. Historically, the Dog Star and Leo are calendrically combined, as they rise together and are intrinsically linked.[1]

Reverence of certain astronomical alignments of Leo, Taurus, and Sirius did not end with the Sumerians. Researchers in the field of alternative archaeology, Graham Hancock and Robert Bauval, have proposed an idea about the relationship between both Leo and Taurus, and the design of the Giza Plateau. They postulate that the Great Pyramid has concavity to its faces. This concavity causes the North face of the pyramid to reflect sunlight in between two specific areas during the year when the Sun is over the Great Pyramid at noon. These two points of light correspond with the position of the Sun in the signs Leo and Taurus in the tropical Zodiac.[2]

These are just a few things to keep in mind as we move along. Later you will see just how advanced the Sumerian's knowledge of the cosmos was, and how it would later influence advancing civilizations like the Egyptians, Greeks, and even *us*.

With all of the changing names, titles, and evolving etymologies, it is easy to see how information about these gods can get so conflated. However, throughout this book, I will do my best to keep it as simple and clear as possible. Now that we know more about what was unearthed in 2013, let's take a look at what was found when archaeologists returned to the site in January of 2014.

Excavations resumed at Tell Khaiber on January 12, 2014, with a larger team than before. This time, eleven British archaeologists worked in the field for nearly three months. As they continued to excavate the primary structure, they learned just how significant this discovery is, describing it as having remarkable symmetry and "a ground plan with no known parallels."[3]

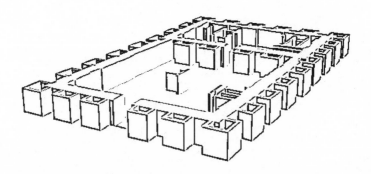

Fig. 1-C: A sketch of the unusual layout of the newly discovered structure. The placement and purpose of all the rooms remain a mystery. There are still more layers to be excavated.

Stop and consider the magnitude of these claims for just a moment. Have you heard of this amazing discovery? Aside from my initial report, *The Sumerian Controversy*, have you seen this covered in any news outlets? Perhaps as an avid archaeology fan, you have seen a blurb or two buried on a few archaeology news sites or blogs. My point is this: How apathetic and cynical have we become as a society that news like this flies under the radar? Is it our fault for being distracted by reality television, sports, or social media?

Maybe the responsibility lies with the project directors. According to their annual report, over half of the allocated budget for the project went to "staff," while only 8% went to promotion.[4] For anyone remotely familiar with fundraising, or business in general, 8% is certainly not enough to gain any significant attention. In the for-profit world, a typical marketing budget would be about 10-20% of projected gross revenues. For non-profits, a typical allocation would be more like 9-12% of the annual organizational budget. Based on these facts, it would appear that this project was never meant to be widely broadcasted.

Thus, it will come as even more of a surprise to learn that when they went back, they found a second building just a short distance away from the administrative center. Although little is yet known about this new building, one thing looks to be true; this area has the potential to become the Sumerian version of the Giza Plateau.

Along with this newly discovered building, fourteen clay tablets were excavated with more still in situ. Many of these tablets are administrative documents like receipts and records of sales, most of which are of grains. Some are short notes, while others are much longer and more complex ledgers. These financial records were housed in one designated room of the building.

Another room contained numerous models made from clay. These models depicted unidentified wheeled vehicles, human figures, and mysterious three-dimensionally shaped objects. If these weren't strange enough, in the North section of the building, the archaeologists were surprised to find an *eye*, made from what they believed to be an early form of glass.

Artifacts were not the only things found. Just as in 2013, a body was found buried in pottery. This time, it was not of an infant, but rather the body of a woman in her late twenties. She was placed in a pair of large pottery jars and then buried in the corner of a room. Around her neck dangled a magnificent necklace comprised of more than fifty imported semi-precious stones. She also wore two beautifully fashioned pins, denoting her relative wealth and status. Who was this woman, and why was she buried in the corner of one of these rooms?

The mystery remains unsolved. Samples of collagen were taken and sent to the University of Liverpool for DNA analysis. Perhaps more will be revealed after the results come in. If so, they will assuredly be buried in the AP newswire.

Latest Developments: 2015

Despite the imminent threat of ISIS/ISIL, archaeologists returned to the Ur region in January of 2015. At the time of writing this book, the project's annual report has not yet been released. However, I can tell you a little bit about what they have found, based on their social media posts.

Aside from additional pottery, statues, and tablets, one artifact stood out, as it had the archaeologists "completely stumped."[5] It is a cylindrical piece made from pottery, standing about 17 ¾ inches high. The piece is sealed at both ends. However, it has three little circular notches in descending order around the middle section of one side (see Fig. 1-D). What could the function of this piece be? We will come back to this and the other artifacts mentioned later.

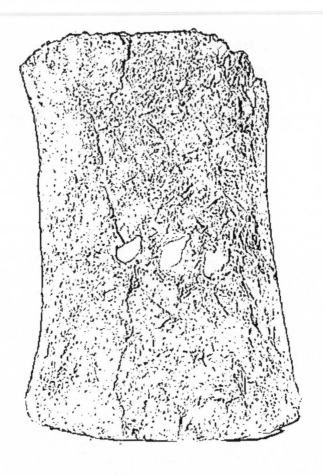

Fig. 1-D

On a side note, I am happy to see that in recent months the project leaders have made a consistent effort to maintain a social media presence. To their credit, as I have always maintained, any lack of transparency about these excavations has not been due to a lack of concern on the part of the archaeologists working at the site. Remember, they are cogs in the machine. The problem lies in the unseen hands that guide (and fund) the machine. While the archeologists do not get a free pass, please keep in mind that they are doing their jobs.

With that all said, why should we care about the hidden hand behind these excavations? Why all of the fuss over the Sumerians? What makes them equally, if not more, enchanting than the Egyptians, Greeks, or even Romans? If these are questions you find yourself wondering, I implore you to read on. This is only the very tip of the iceberg.

CIVILIZATION RISING

*"The end of the human race will be that it will
eventually die of civilization."*
—Ralph Waldo Emerson

The Puzzle of Human Origins

Some have suggested that the Sumerians
should be researched more thoroughly because
they were the first people. However, this is not
true. Homo sapiens, meaning "man who knows,"
in Latin, is the scientific name for the general human species. Homo is the genus, or, taxonomic
category that is positioned above species and below family. This includes Neanderthals and Den-
isovan, as well as many other of our extinct cous-
ins. In fact, Homo sapiens is the only surviving
species of the genus Homo. Modern humans are
classified even further as the subspecies, Homo
sapiens sapiens. This classification system
branches out further and further whenever a new
specimen is found. Sometimes, a specimen that
does not neatly fit into this ongoing jig saw puzzle
gets conveniently forgotten in the basements of

museums; museums funded by oligarchs (see Fig. 2-A).

Even a public display can show how sorted the question of human origin is. The pictures in Figs. 2-B—2-E are the typical tourist's view from the Smithsonian's display on the human family fossil record. This is by no means a full record or complete scientific analysis, as you will see. It is just a tiny glimpse at what is presented as fact by virtue of it being displayed to the everyday public of school children, families, and vacationers. In my opinion, displays like these, while indeed interesting and important, are not benefitting the public as much as they are benefitting the academic community, and as this book will argue, corporate elites.

Fig. 2-A: Hall of Human Origins, Smithsonian museum in Washington, D.C.. Funded by one of the infamous Koch Brothers. (Photo Credit: Dr. Heather Lynn)

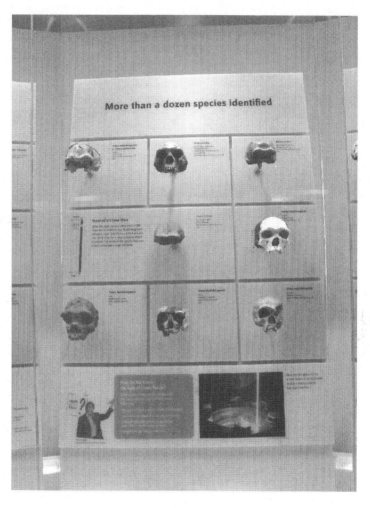

Fig. 2-B

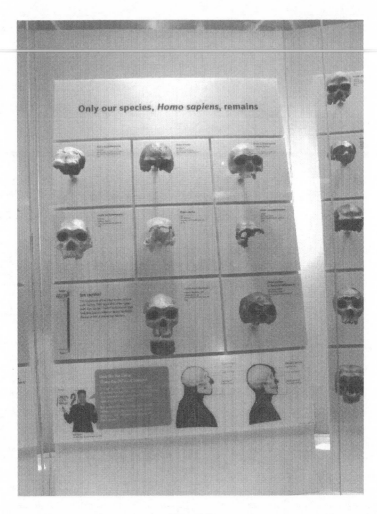

Fig. 2-C

Fig. 2-D

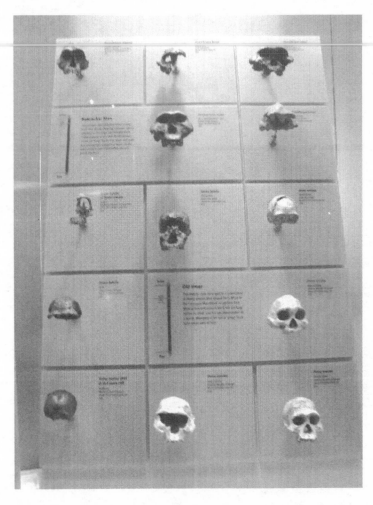

Fig. 2-E

Now, you may argue according to your religious beliefs, or personal research theories, that these "ancestors" are of no relation to us modern humans, thus, their existence does not factor into the equation. To which I would point to the Omo remains, discovered between 1967 and 1974 in Africa, at the Omo Kibish sites near the Omo River, in Omo National Park in south-western Ethiopia.

Found at the site were a number of bones including, two partial skulls, four jaws, a leg bone, and about two hundred teeth. This discovery provided evidence of the first anatomically modern humans appearing in the fossil record about 195,000 years ago. This fits nicely within the time frame scientists claim modern humans diverged from a common ancestor about 200,000 years ago. If the radiocarbon dating is correct, these fossils are the oldest known Homo sapiens remains, "making Ethiopia the cradle of Homo sapiens."[6]

Ethiopia may be considered the cradle of Homo sapiens, but Mesopotamia, home of Sumer, is known as the cradle of civilization. The distinction is quite important. Existing and civilization building are two very different things. However, one could then reasonably ask what about Göbekli Tepe? Evidence found at Göbekli Tepe clearly indicates more than just simple existing was taking place. Considering that the settlement is at least

11,000 years old, it is much older than any settlement found near Ur. Thus, the enigmatic inhabitants of Göbekli Tepe should be considered the cradle of civilization, but the problem with this is how one defines civilization.

Some scholars adhere to the theory that Göbekli Tepe was a temple, but not all scholars agree. Archaeological evidence of day to day activities have led other scholars to believe that Göbekli Tepe was a multi-purpose domestic settlement. Still, the general consensus is that Göbekli Tepe was a hunter-gather site with the possibility of rudimentary agriculture. Does this constitute civilization? Perhaps it is the seed of civilization but to date, no evidence of an advanced state of human society where a high level of culture, science, industry, and government has been found.

This is not to suggest that Göbekli Tepe is not a profoundly important site to the history of humanity. After all, its mysteries have only begun to be addressed. I only mean to suggest that in Sumer, something different happened. This *something* would do more than simply plant the seeds of human civilization, it would lead the Sumerians to developing complex systems and hierarchies, such as the world had never seen.

While not the first ever people, and not the first to make art or large settlements, the Sumerians forever changed the trajectory of humankind. Thanks to having invented the world's first true system of writing, the Sumerians have left us with many artifacts and texts to paint a picture of life in their time. [7] Their meticulous record keeping has allowed us to study their culture in great detail, of which some has yet to be interpreted. So what do we really know about the Sumerians? What made their version of civilization so different than in prehistory, and what makes it so similar to our modern version of civilization?

Who were the Sumerians?

Before the rise of the Sumerian civilization, complex and primitive societies alike were formed by hunter-gatherers. Hunter-gather settlements, such as Göbekli Tepe, Çatalhöyük, and even Stonehenge, show evidence of feasting, dancing, celebrating, *and* spirituality. Evidence points to these early societies as being both egalitarian and non-combative. In other words, these settlements were peaceful domiciles with no distinct social class divisions. Researchers suggest this may be due to factors such as the inhabitants' communal lifestyle, interdependence on one another, lack of individual property ownership, absence of individual wealth or status, and the mere fact they could not hoard wealth or commodities. Thus, people lived for the day, shared with one another, and valued each other's contribution to their settlement.

This all changed in what seems like an instant when the Sumerians appeared. The discovery of the Sumerians rattled pre-existing ideas about the rise of human civilization. Who were these people, and why had they been left out of the archaeological and historical record for over 2000 years?[8]

Scholars describe the Sumerians as exhibiting an "unusually creative intellect."[9] By at least the fourth millennium BCE, the first urban center formed. These early civilizations began with the Sumerians and would later include the Akkadians, Babylonians, and Assyrians. In Mesopotamia, the area between the Tigris and Euphrates rivers (modern day Iraq), there was an instantaneous boom of cultural development.

In a mere 300 years (a historical blink of an eye) huge complex structures, theology, technologies, and governments emerged. Inventions unlike anything the world had ever known began to manifest and would forever change the course of human culture. Such high levels of civilization were responsible for creating a more unified culture in the region; the seeds of homogeny and pop culture. What this mean, is that every single day, we are benefitting from some aspect of the Sumerians ingenuity.

Here is a just a portion of inventions and technologies with which the Sumerians are credited:[10] [11]

- The invention of time
- Astronomy
- A system of numbers
- Weights and measure
- Mathematics
- Geometry
- The 360 degree circle
- The wheel
- Wheeled vehicles
- Sailboats
- Maps
- Harnessing the wind for power
- Many agricultural developments such as irrigation
- Animal domestication
- Aquariums
- The concept of an end to the work or school day
- Labor Unions
- Surgery
- Dentistry
- Optometry
- Pharmaceuticals (including pills)
- Credit and financing
- A bicameral Congress (a Congress composed of two separate chambers, a Senate and the House of Representatives)
- Libraries

- Schools and universities
- The concept of professional careers
- Clergy
- Historians
- Economists
- Philosophers
- Teachers
- Lawyers
- Politicians
- Bankers

As you can see, these inventions are not your average stone tool, arrow head, or mud hut. These are all teachable skills, rooted in a deeper, more conceptual way of thinking. What happened to make this shift in thinking and doing?

Fig. 2-F: Sumerian mathematics tablet. Originally owned by corporate financier and industrialist, J. P. Morgan. He later gave the artifact to Yale University.

Current theories propose that increased competition for resources created a need for more workers. This new working class needed managers, leading to a development of a state superstructure, or *government*. Subsequently, the bureaucracy introduced by this new government system would need a supporting physical structure, like temples and administrative centers, like the one purportedly found near Ur.

Furthermore, the increased centralization of economic activity demanded the development of more detailed methods of record keeping thus giving rise to the invention of writing, math, and so forth. Who would be able to do these activities? To solve this new problem, schools were developed to train a specialized workforce. People were then trained as scribes, managers, skilled craftsman, builders, physicians, scientists, priests, and others at high levels of government. By now, a complete transition from clan or tribal law to a more recognizable modern state governance occurred. This shift is often referred to as the "Urban Revolution."

Interestingly, the word urban comes from the Latin *urbanus*, meaning "of or pertaining to a city or city life." It is from urbs (genitive urbis), meaning "city, walled town," of which this term is of unknown origin.[12] Could there be a linguistic connection to Ur, Uruk, etc., that would connect the generative Latin origin of the term for city to that of the earliest cities known? This would really give a new dimension to the term *Ur*ban Revolution!

As a scholar of history, I believe the Urban Revolution to be the most likely explanation for the abrupt rise in high civilization. However, after publishing my previous report, I have spoken with some interesting people; people who would go on to open my eyes to a number of *alternative* theories surrounding the Sumerians. These experiences have forever changed the way I approach research.

THROUGH THE LOOKING GLASS

"But I don't want to go among mad people," Alice remarked.
"Oh, you can't help that," said the Cat: "we're all mad here. I'm mad. You're mad."
"How do you know I'm mad?" said Alice.
"You must be," said the Cat, "or you wouldn't have come here."

—Lewis Carroll
Alice's Adventures in Wonderland

My Journey Begins

After the release of *The Sumerian Controversy*, I was inundated with emails and letters proposing various theories and ideas about the Sumerian people, their technology, and why the corporate elite are so interested in Sumerian history and artifacts that they would fund archaeological excavations.

As a result, I had the opportunity to meet with interesting researchers, everyday people, and whistleblowers. Ultimately, this led to meetings via the dark web, a Hollywood gathering which could only be compared to Stanly Kubrick's movie, *Eyes Wide Shut*, and a host of security, hacking, and safety issues for me. However, the information I uncovered has forced me to reconsider everything I ever thought true. The following are a selection of meetings and experiences I had while investigating alternative theories that were brought to me. Please be advised that some of what you are about to read is a personal account of my experiences while researching and not scientific research.

Bill, the Retiree

"What am I looking at here?"

"Don't you see? It is the missing piece of the puzzle." said Bill.

Big bulbous head, black almond eyes; everything you'd come to expect when looking at the body of an extraterrestrial.

"Is this it, or is there more?" I asked, carefully reaching back into the manila envelope. I pulled out an unmarked DVD case. My heart dropped. It appeared to be a boot-legged copy of Steven Spielberg's, *Close Encounters of the Third Kind*.

"No. There's more...lots more." Bill responded, staring deep into my eyes. "Sorry to keep asking you, Dr. Lynn, but I gotta be sure. Were you followed here?"

"I said I wanted a grande size!" a child's voice screeched.

I gasped, after having been hit by a sticky wash of hot chocolate.

"Sorry!" muttered a tall, red-headed, overburdened woman in black yoga capris and large tortoise shell sunglasses. The purple monarch butterfly tattoo on her pale calf was so vividly colored, it seemed to have dimension.

"That's quite alright." I uttered, but the woman didn't respond. She hurried over to the barista, checkbook in hand, ready to purchase another hot chocolate for her little screaming daughter. I caught a glimpse at Bill. He looked like he'd seen a ghost.

"I think that's my cue to leave. Thank you for your time, Dr. Lynn. I hope you've found these documents useful to your research."

Never taking his eyes off of the tall woman and her demanding toddler, Bill slowly rose from his seat and started walking to the coffee shop door.

"Wait, Bill! We can go somewhere a little less crowded. I think there's..."

"We've already been discovered!" he inter-rupted. "I would suggest you wait a few minutes, then leave after me."

I traveled over 300 miles for an old DVD and to meet with yet another UFO guy. What on Earth would UFOs have to do with archaeology, anyway?

Old Professor Shaftner

I was once told by a professor in an under-graduate class on the anthropology of war, that the most important thing every good archaeologist brings with them into the field is a bottle of hard liquor. He then went on to proclaim that, "few indigenous people can resist a stiff drink." Archaeology is sometimes an alcohol-fueled profession, at least in the Western part of the world. I tend to avoid alcohol except for the occasional glass of red wine, so I have not experienced this first hand. However, it always struck me as an ethnocentric, and even colonialist view on indigenous people.

Thus, I should not have been surprised to learn that Professor Jon Shaftner was no stranger to spirits. I suspect he may have been slightly in-toxicated the first time I met him. It was a damp fall morning at the natural history museum's Archaeology Day; a day designed to bring public awareness, interest, and involvement to archaeology. In reality, it ended up as a haven for home-schooled kindergartners and their overly stressed helicopter moms.

As I perused the tables and had obligatory small talk with some old colleagues and professors, I caught a glimpse of a man in a bright white fedora. He looked familiar. *Richard Attenborough!*

He looked just like Richard Attenborough's character in the first Jurassic Park movie. Amused, I went over to his table to introduce myself.

"Excuse me." I said.

"Yes? Hello! Can you believe this shit?" Professor Shaftner asked.

Speechless, I couldn't help but to raise my eyebrows in searching for how to respond.

"I mean, they couldn't even give me an assistant? I am pushing 75 and they expect me to drag all of this rubbish around like some sort of dog and pony show. Well let me tell you, they are just looking for any way to get me out so that they can redirect what sorry excuse for a budget I have to the medical anthropology program. It's always about the money and never about the discovery! Don't forget that! It's just like Afghanistan. Do you know about Afghanistan?"

Standing up, Professor Shaftner leaned in close to me and whispered, "No one knows the truth about Afghanistan. They've made sure of that. Why do you think we went to war?"

I caught a whiff of alcohol on his breath. What had I walked in to?

"*Well*, do you know why we went to war?" Professor Shaftner demanded.

"Oil?" I asked.

"Ha! Everyone thinks it's oil. It's such a convenient distraction. It really is. Can you believe they make me sit out here with all of these brochures and adverts? They know my department is being systematically destroyed. I think they get some sort of pleasure having me drag all these things out here by myself. 'Oh! Go on there, old man, and set up your dog and pony show and don't forget to bring your bag of tricks for the kiddies!' He said, mockingly.

"I used to have so many graduate assistants. Now, I have no one. I have to wash my own artifacts. Well you know what? I don't! I refuse. I simply refuse..."

At this point I realized this was going nowhere. As I stood there listening to his ramblings, I tried to find a break in the conversation to graciously excuse myself.

"Well, it was nice meeting you..." I smiled and grabbed a printed brochure before waving goodbye. Slowly turning away from Professor Shaftner's table, I heard him mutter something under his breath. I smiled and asked, "What was that?"

"You heard me." he grumbled.

"No, I'm afraid I didn't." I insisted.

"Puppet! You're a puppet! Go on now little puppet! Back to your table, puppet! They're pulling your strings again!"

"Excuse me?" I asked indignantly, lowering my voice as to not cause a scene. "If I'm a puppet, then what are you? You're doing the same thing here that I'm doing!"

"Don't you see, then? We're both puppets! Ha!" said Professor Shaftner with a hearty laugh. He abruptly got quiet, walked out from behind the table and leaned in close. With the most serious look in his eyes he said, "All the world's a puppet show and the strings are pulled by giants."

His icy-blue gaze left me a bit unsettled. I asked what he meant by "giants." Not breaking his gaze, he slowly leaned back and said, "You know...like, *Goliath*."

"Jack and the Beanstalk Giants?" I drolled.

"Don't be ridiculous girl! I mean Nephilim. For Christ's sake, didn't you pay attention in Sunday school?"

"Maybe you could enlighten me sometime." I suggested.

"Maybe you could help me pack up this dog and pony show? There's not enough room in my car for it all." With a wink, he reached into his front shirt pocket, grabbed a pair of gold aviator sunglasses and started walking to the entrance of the museum. He turned back, gave a thumbs up and yelled, "I'll pull the wagon around front!" His voice echoed through the main lobby.

46

Oddly intrigued, I gathered the old man's artifacts and displays and ran to my car, clutching loose papers and a display case of small artifacts. As I arranged the supplies in the back of my truck, I heard a loud rumble of a loose exhaust approaching. I look over to see a little green Prius sputtering along. It was Professor Shaftner. With a cigarette between is lips he asks, "Is my table cleared off?"

"No. Not yet. I just broke it down and I was going back in for your..."

"Just get in!" he demanded.

"But I haven't completely broken down your table yet." I protested.

"Screw it!" yelled the professor as his laugh gave way to a wet, productive cough.

I hurried over to his wagon and got in. He glanced at my brown leather, knee-high boots and asked if I wore "those things" in the field. I told him I did not but was not sure if he had heard me, as he didn't respond. Instead, he turned up his stereo and started singing along to some strange psychedelic music. Between the sounds of rock organ and bass guitar, an exotic voice rang out in a traditional Middle Eastern scale. It was so different. It sounded like nothing I'd ever heard before.

"Far out isn't it?" Professor Shaftner asked. "Who am I kidding? By the look of those boots,

47

you're probably more in to that Lady Goo Goo stuff."

"I think you mean Lady Ga Ga, but no. I am more of a classical music fan.

"Why?"

"Hmmm...I don't know, really. Maybe because I play French horn. I guess I've just always loved it, even as a kid."

My body suddenly lunged forward, as the professor slammed his brakes. We were in the middle of the road. He looks over at me and asks, "What happens when the cultural symbols you love are destroyed?"

Still reeling, I moved my hair away from my face and just looked at him, blankly.

"Listen to this. It's more than just music. It's the sound of a beautiful and prosperous Afghanistan. The artist is Ahmad Zahir. He was considered the King of Afghani pop music during the 60s and 70s. He was like Elvis; big star. Unfortunately, he was killed in 1979 by the order of a communist general who hated Ahmad's music because of its political lyrics, which were at odds with the communist government of the time. What a loss. What a great loss. A graduate assistant of mine once took my old tapes and somehow got them on to these CDs."

The honking of car horns heightened my awareness of our surroundings. We were sitting in the middle of the road.

"Maybe we should get to where we're going, and then talk about this in greater detail." I sheepishly suggested.

"You think I'm reckless don't you?" Professor Shaftner asked.

Not wanting to offend him, I told him no. For about the next five miles he behaved. We finally pulled into the driveway of a rundown duplex-style house.

"Well, here we are!"

Upon entering, I was surprised at how beautifully decorated Professor Shaftner's home was. I guess I figured that it would look as disorderly as he acted. Boy was I wrong. The walls were covered in art from every culture and civilization you could imagine. The rugs looked as though they were taken right out of a sultan's palace.

"What do you drink?"

"Water, no ice, thank you." I responded.

"Your lips said water but your boots say vodka."

I smiled, and as the ornery old professor went into the kitchen. He came out with our drinks and we sat down at his huge mahogany table.

"What were you saying earlier about David and Goliath?" I asked.

The professor looked up from his drink, and asked, "Did you know that Sumer is the Land of the Watchers? Have you ever wondered who the Watchers are?"

"You mean, who the Watchers *were*?" I corrected.

He reached into his shirt pocket and pulled out a pen.

"Take notes. I'm about to teach you what I am not allowed to teach my students."

The hours ticked on and eventually night fell. I listened to everything Professor Shaftner said. I even took notes. We discussed his beliefs that the Sumerian people lived among giants, or Nephilim. We even discussed his belief that these Nephilim were ancient astronauts. Perhaps the most interesting discussions revolved around his time spent living in Afghanistan. He was happy to repeat the story about how, as a graduate student, he had the pleasure of dining with Mohammed Zahir Shah, the last King of Afghanistan, who reigned for from 1933 until he was ousted by a Soviet-backed Communist coup in 1973.

I would go on to meet with him once a week to discuss his past, experiences, and theories on, of all things, ancient "astronauts." The last time we

50

met was close to the holidays. It was then that he showed me a small piece of a tablet. He claimed that it was definitive proof that "we came from them," as he put it. The tablet fragment was only about a 4cm x 6cm. He said it was from approximately 2600–2350 BCE, found at Nippur. I asked him what made this tablet so compelling. He grew strangely sullen, and replied:

"You, and everyone will see soon enough. Once I piece it all together, I will show the world. To me, this isn't some little project, it's my *destiny*."

I was determined to find out what was on the tablet, and why he had it at his home under lock and key, rather than at the university. I thought maybe he was waiting until he felt he could truly trust me before he'd let me examine the tablet fragment. So, I continued with my weekly visits until one day, in December when no one answered the door.

Soon, all contact with Professor Shaftner stopped. He would not return my calls or emails. The few times I would stop by, he wasn't home; at least he didn't answer, nor was his car in his driveway. I hesitated in calling the university. I felt that maybe I was starting to be worried for

51

nothing. It had only been a few weeks of no contact.

The holidays came and went; still no sign of the old professor. We had a break in the snow and the sun finally came out, so I decided I would just drive by and take a look. As I slowly drove by his duplex, I noticed a few cars in the driveway. My curiosity got the best of me. I parked and knocked on the front door.

A tall woman with red hair came to the door.

"Hello. May I help you?" she asked.

"Maybe. I'm looking for Dr. Jon Shaftner. Is he home?"

"No. I'm sorry. He's no longer with us." She said, her voice quivering.

"Is he…"

"Yes. He passed a few months ago. We are just here going through a few of his things and cleaning up the place. We're getting it ready for the new tenants."

As she spoke, I could see into the professor's home. The walls, now barren, showed the golden nicotine outlines of where his pictures and art once were. *The tablet.*

"I'm sorry for your loss. It looks like you've had a lot of things to go through. Professor Shaftner had a lot of unique collectibles from his travels. I don't mean to be so forward, but have you contacted the university to perhaps donate some of his artifacts? If not, I would be more than happy to make arrangements on your behalf." My motives were two-fold.

"Are you one of his graduate students?" she retorted.

"No, I'm a colleague. My name is Dr. Heather Lynn. I was working on a project with him." I quickly responded.

"I don't mean to be rude, Dr. Lynn, but I am tired of all these people clamoring over Jon's stuff. His body was still warm when they came for his archaeology junk. They're like vultures."

"Who?" I asked. "The university?"

"I really don't know. I just assumed they were from the university. They were in suits and they brought vans. I figured Jon must have made arrangements ahead of time for something like this." she replied.

"Were you here when this happened? Did you have to sign anything? Did you happened to get any names?" I said with increasing desperation.

"I'm sorry Dr. Lynn, I'm not sure I understand what you are implying. What do…"

"Kelly, who is at the door?" said a dark haired gentleman.

Before she could answer, the dark haired man came over, put his arm around the woman and told her she needed to go lie down. He said nothing to me. He just glared at me as he shut the front door of the house.

The red haired woman never even put up a fight. She just let this man shuffle her along in the middle of our conversation.

Baffled, I went home. I called the university to inquire about their retrieval of Dr. Shaftner's artifacts and was told that Dr. Shaftner had retired years ago. I asked if he had still been affiliated with their archaeology program. They said no. He no longer taught, kept office hours, or had affiliation. Then, I called the local museum to inquire about the artifacts. They were even less helpful. To this very day, I have no idea what happened to the professor's private collection of Sumerian tablets.

Derek the Soldier

"Thank you for coming all this way to meet with me, Dr. Lynn. When I read your report, I knew you were the only person who'd listen to what I have to say."

"I'm happy to be here, but first let me say, thank you for your service." I responded.

Derek's eyes quickly shot down into a distant gaze.

"No disrespect, but every time I hear that, I just wonder if anyone knows what they are really thanking me for. No one on the other side can ever really understand. I think they only say it to alleviate civilian guilt. It's really just self-serving."

My cheeks flushed. "That makes sense. Please accept my apology, then."

"When I read your email, I was intrigued. What can you tell me about the looting of Iraq's National Museum in Baghdad? You stated that there was nothing accidental about it, but that it was a carefully strategized operation. Can you elaborate on this?"

Leaning back, Derek said, "Just think about it for a minute. Had the place been looted by local peasants, the artifacts that were easier to carry would have been gone first; things like jewelry, tablets, little statues...you know, stuff like that. Those things could have been bagged up quickly and then sold on the black market. That's not what happened, though."

"It isn't" I asked.

"This entire thing could easily have been stopped, but the Pentagon ignored the warnings. Did you know that the American administration refused to provide security for Baghdad's museums, even after they had been warned over and over again by officials?"

"I had heard some rumors of the sort." I offered.

Derek's voice lowered as he leaned closer.

"The looters were smart enough to know which exhibits had replicas. They passed right by the fakes. These looters were hired professionals. Not only did they know to take the real artifacts, they were able to remove extremely heavy statues, meaning they had heavy equipment. They didn't even have to break in to the storage rooms because, well, they had the keys! These guys were looking for very specific treasures and knew right where to look."

"What were they looking for?" I asked.

Derek paused. He leaned a bit closer and whispered, "I know they were looking for very specific things. I know they took a certain gold vessel that was discovered at Ur."

"May I ask how you know these things, Derek?"

"It was late one night and some British guy claiming to be a journalist gave my unit a map and tried to convince us to literally run into a burning building to save these artifacts. He said the building was burning fast; that the flames were shooting over 200 feet into the sky. The smoke could be seen from miles away. The man was escorted off of the base and we just stayed behind wondering what was going on. I really wanted to help. I could actually see the smoke in the distance. I kept thinking that this was another burning, just like the one at Alexandria at that library. There wasn't anything we could do."

I could sense that Derek felt helpless.

"I know there is more to this, Dr. Lynn."

"Please, call me Heather."

"Heather, they are looking for something. They are looking for *technologies*."

"Technologies." I echoed. "What technologies? Things like, the Bagdad Battery? I suggested.

"Things like *stargates*." Derek mused. "I know it sounds hard to believe, but I saw it for myself."

"Please go on." I begged.

"On my initial deployment to Afghanistan, I encountered an elderly couple in a village. The man was eager to show me a hole near his house. It looked like the opening to an underground storm shelter, but it had a stone covering, rather than wood. His wife was very upset that he was showing me. I thought it was a shelter, but the man told me that it had been there long before them. He went on to warn that anyone who went into the hole would come out on the other side of the world."

"You mean like, the proverbial hole to China?" I quipped.

"No, like for real, like a teleportation device. The Afghani man went on to explain that his wife did not want me to know because they didn't want to lose their home or worse, be killed."

"Why would they be killed over showing you a storm shelter?" I asked.

"Well for one, it was no storm shelter. The wife was afraid there had been military raids on properties like theirs, where these stone covered holes had been located."

"Isn't it possible that these military officials were simply trying to find enemy hiding places?" I asked, as Derek pulled an electronic cigarette from his shirt pocket.

"*We* are the enemy." He said shaking his head.

"What do you mean?" I asked.

"We are fighting a proxy war" He exclaimed.

Derek's face disappeared behind a fruit scented cloud.

"A proxy war between the U.S. and Russia, so I've heard." I agreed.

"No. That's only one layer. It's completely compartmentalized to cover the fact that it is a proxy war between super wealthy families. They are at war with each other and have been for years. It goes back to what they are doing in the Middle East all together."

I started "Which is...?"

"They are looking for a tablet that will give them power over everyone on Earth. I know this because I have a few buddies who got recruited in a *destiny project*."

A chill went down my arm as a rush of warmth flooded my stomach.

The Tablet of Destinies

Derek and I spoke for another thirty minutes or so. As he proceeded to analyze and explain various aspects of the science fiction film franchise, *Stargate*, I couldn't help but think about Bill and his belief in the movie, *Close Encounters of the Third Kind*. Both men spoke about these films as though they were documentaries of actual events.

Films like these clearly have an effect on people. They provide a context for which to explain the unexplainable. I couldn't help but wonder what Bill, Professor Shaftner, and Derek had in common. I found myself trying to find a common thread between these folks. Could their economic or social standings have influenced their beliefs? Perhaps they had all endured trauma or some level of hardship which left them feeling disenfranchised. Maybe they were all somehow wronged by "the system," hence, drawn into a paranoid subculture where science fiction films seemed all too real. Whatever the case, I believed there was inherent value in what they were telling me.

After a continued series of meetings with whistleblowers and independent scholars, I ventured down a new path of research. I would begin to discover just who these "Watchers" were, what role they played in history, and what role they could still be playing. I began doubting my own previously held beliefs. My research would go on to support a lot of the testimony I received, with each discovery pushing me closer to the boundaries of reason. So who were the *Watchers*, and where did they come from?

THE WATCHERS

"All of us are watchers – of television, of time clocks, of traffic on the freeway – but few are observers. Everyone is looking, not many are seeing."

—Peter M. Leschak

Primordial Beginnings

In 1849, archaeologist, politician, and *Knight Grand Cross of the Order of the Bath*, Sir Austen Henry Layard, excavated Nimrud and Nineveh, and went on to discover the Royal Library of Ashurbanipal, in 1851.

Ashurbanipal was the last great king of the Neo-Assyrian Empire. The 'Ashur' in his name, means the creator of an heir. This powerful king was known also in Greek writings as Sardanapalus and as Asnappeer, or Osnapper (Asenappar), in the Bible (Ezra 4:10).

Fig. 4-A: Sir Austen Henry Layard (1817-1894)

Fig. 4-B: Assurbanipal riding and hunting. Relief carving from the north palace of Nineveh, ca. 640 BCE. (British Museum)

Fig. 4-C: Artist depiction of the Library of Assurbanipal

Both Persian and Armenian lore recount that Alexander the Great had such deep admiration for the Royal Library of Ashurbanipal at Nineveh, that he made it his life's goal to build one just as grand, if not grander. This, led to the creation of Alexander's own famous library, the Library of Alexandria. So why was Ashurbanipal's library so awe-inspiring?

The Royal Library of Ashurbanipal contained thousands of clay tablets (mostly fragments) with various texts dating as far back as the 7th century BCE, including the famous poem, the *Epic of Gilgamesh*. Layard unearthed many tablet fragments which told variations of the Babylonian *Legend of the Deluge* and of the *Creation*. The texts on fragments of the First and Fifth Tablets of Creation describe the fight between the "Gods and Chaos." The third tablet described the "Fall of Man."

Scholars are still trying to decipher all that was found at the site because those who handled the original artifacts left them a scattered mess. Fragments of tablets now sit in museum archives like puzzle pieces in a nine-year-old's bedroom. There is no telling what more we have to learn from these rare documents. Could some of these hold the key to understanding human origins?

Luckily, there were a number of texts which had survived in their original form, including the ancient creation myth, Enûma Eliš (Enuma Elish). This text has nearly one thousand lines of cuneiform script recorded over seven clay tablets, each holding between 115 and 170. It is one of the most important texts to our understanding of religious origins. The recitation in itself was a ceremonial ritual and celebration. You can find the complete epic online by searching for translation by Assyriologist and historian, W.G. Lambert.

In the beginning, according to these seven tablets, nothing existed, except Abzu, the primal being made of fresh water. Abzu was mostly described as a boundless, confused and disordered mass of watery matter. Out of this "living water" came two distinct types of beings; demons and gods. The demons took on the appearance of animal/human amalgamations and were described as terrifying. By contrast, the gods had unblemished human-like forms.

These gods represented a dimensional trinity: the heavens, the atmosphere, and the underworld. However, the atmosphere and the underworld were bound together, creating what we now as Earth. This was set in opposition to the heavens, creating what could arguably be seen as the first great duality of mankind.

Abzu would form a union with Tiamat, the primordial goddess of the ocean, represented as salt water, in contrast to Abzu's freshwater. The first god to be created from this union was Lahmu. Lahmu means "parent star or constellation." He would later have a sister named, Laḫamu. They would become the parents of Anshar (*An* = heaven, *shár* = horizon, end) and Kishar, whose name means whole earth. These deities were the sky father and earth mother, who would go on to create the gods of the Mesopotamian Pantheon through the "mixing of their waters."

This Pantheon would include, Anu (from the Sumerian, *An*, meaning sky), Anu was referred to as the God of Heaven, Lord of the Constellations, Spirits and Demons, and King of Kings, among other equally grand titles. It was believed that Anu would judge the sins on Earth and if he determined there was an injustice, or crime committed, he would create "star soldiers" to come down and destroy the evildoers.

Fig. 4-D: Cuneiform character, DINGIR. Used to represent, Anu. Meaning "heavens" or "deity."

The Anunnaki

Anu would go on to procreate. Anu, as the father god, beget Enki and Enil, with whom he would later be syncretized. Enki is often described in very real, biological terms, whereas Enil is described as a spirit, or "Lord Ghost." The Sumerian word "líl", whose Akkadian equivalent is zaqīqu, means "ghost, phantom, haunted" (Michalowski 1989: 98; Tinney 1996: 129-30; Michalowski 1998). Some scholars argue that this cannot be a correct translation, because it does not seem to make sense in the context of his mythological capabilities. However, what does stand out in this context is the likely Sumerian origins of a paternal trinity comprised of a heavenly father, son, and holy ghost; all of whom had equal but shared power over humanity.

These were the main three deities. Still, Anu would go on to create more progeny. The subsequent children of Anu would become known as, the *Anunnaki*. It is unclear as to whether or not the Anunnaki were true gods. Details surrounding this mysterious group are scattered. In fact, no one knows for sure just how many Anunnaki there were in total. One text suggests that there are about 50, while another refers to only seven. An entirely separate account describes how Marduk assigned 300 Anunnaki gods for duty in the heavens, and 300 the netherworld, thus, totaling 600 Anunnaki beings.

The main purpose of these beings, as described in the Sumerian myth, *Enki and the World Order*, was to decide the fate of man. They are also described as residing in the netherworld. Many modern popular accounts depict the Anunnaki as having been worshipped. While this could make some sort of logical sense, there is no hard evidence for their worship in the archaeological record, with the exception of only three attestations in administrative texts from the Ur III period, in which it hints that offerings were made to Anunna (Anunnaki).

Sumer has been called, the *Land of the Watchers*. Is it the Anunnaki that are watching? According to the book of Enoch, the "Watchers" were what Abrahamic religions call, the Nephilim. They were the result of the interbreeding of Anunnaki and mankind.

"When the sons of men had multiplied, in those days, beautiful and comely daughters were born to them. And the watchers, the sons of heaven, saw them and desired them. And they said to one another, 'Come, let us choose for ourselves wives from the daughters of men, and let us beget children for ourselves.'"

—The Book of Enoch 6:1

Now, many have heard of the Anunnaki, either from mainstream academic accounts, or popular media. These beings and their related myths rose to prominence after being presented by the author Zecharia Sitchin in his book, *The 12th Planet*. It was this book, as well as subsequent works, that presented an alternative cosmology to the Anunnaki mythology. Sitchin is to some extent, a controversial figure. Most scholars discount his interpretations of Sumerian tablets as pseudoscience. Others, respect him for his passion and dedication, as well as bringing the Sumerians myths to the masses.

Fig. 4-E: Zecharia Sitchin (1920-2010)

In a nutshell, Sitchin claims that there was an extraterrestrial component to Sumerian myths, which would go on to shape human history. According to Sitchin, there is a yet to be discovered planet called Nibiru, positioned beyond Neptune. It follows an elliptical orbit reaching the inner solar system roughly every 3,600 years. Nibiru collided with Tiamat, however in this account, Tiamat is not the goddess previously mentioned, but rather another planet, once located between Mars and Jupiter. The results of this catastrophic event, were the formation of Earth, the asteroid belt, and the comets. Sitchin suggests that during the collision, the planet Tiamat divided into two parts, one of which struck Nibiru, becoming the asteroid belt. The other part was then struck by one of Nibiru's moons, pushing it into a new orbit. That second half would become planet Earth as we know it today.

Nibiru, was supposedly home to a technologically advanced human-like race of giants called the Anunnaki. Sitchin's theory is that these beings came to Earth looking for gold, which they needed to preserve their own atmosphere. Sitchin wrote that Enki suggested that a new race should be created in order to alleviate the Anunnaki of some of the physical demands of mining. Hence, he created robust primitive workers through genetic manipulation, making Homo sapiens the slave species of the gods. Enki did this by splicing extraterrestrial genes with the genes of Homo erectus.

Furthermore, Sitchin, believed that ancient texts describe Sumer as being set up as sort of a colony under the watchful eyes of these Anunnaki overlords. Human kingship was then developed as a type of "middle-management" system to mediate between mankind and the Anunnaki. This would have been the first doctrine of the "divine right of kings" that would go on to be the doctrine under which all monarchy would use.

Before going on, I must qualify my position. I am often asked about my personal feelings on Sitchin and/or whether or not I believe his interpretations. While some people will cringe when I say this, I must stay true to my convictions, just as Sitchin did to his.

I enjoy Sitchin's work. I am intrigued by his romanticism and I am supremely interested in the overall themes. However, having studied Sumerian creation myths as well as a variety of other texts with the hope of finding some unifying themes, which I have, I must conclude that the Sitchin account is not entirely accurate or complete. After speaking with people in elite social circles, many of whom subscribe to similar beliefs, I have come to find a parallel theory about the Anunnaki, and what type of beings they actually are; light-beings who act as the hidden hand in history, guiding the trajectory of our planet and its inhabitant.

I believe Sitchin and his predecessors, Immanuel Velikovsky and Erich von Däniken, have brought to light some interesting ways of looking at myths, artifacts, and society as a whole. I think there is an underlying truth to their vision, yet I think that term "extraterrestrial" now unfortunately conjures up images of little green men, retro or outdated technology, and basically science fiction.

Based on my research, I would be more apt to say that these beings were not extraterrestrial biological entities, as Sitchin and others may describe, but rather, beings on some higher plane, or vibration. The Sumerian records actually refer to these beings as being interdimensional. This could explain why they "come from the heavens." I disagree that these beings would have needed spaceships and the like. If they were truly as advanced as the Sumerians claimed, they would have no need for 1960s or 70s style aeronautics.

Again, this is not to suggest that Sitchin was wrong, as some would argue. I think that Sitchin's work should be a springboard for new ideas. It would be wholly irresponsible for us to progress through time and technology and not expand on his work because we were too busy staunchly adhering to old ways of thinking. Just as I wouldn't only accept the word of any one professor, I would not accept the word of any one author. This is the realm of the guru, not the scholar. Gurus are meant to be followed. Scholars are meant to be challenged, and their work built upon. By unquestionably subscribing to the teachings of one person, no matter the person is, is putting that person as a guru or even cult leader (the cult of personality).

Sitichin wanted to be taken seriously. He wanted his work to be viewed as scholarship, not cult rantings. To hold his work to a lower standard of academic scholarship would not be honoring his work, or his memory. For Sitchin's work to be considered scholarly, it does not need to have taken place in a traditional academic setting. However, it does need to go through an empirical process, which is what I try to do. It is as Carl Sagan once said about standing on the shoulders of giants. Even that comment was a derivative quote of

Isaac Newton in a letter to his rival Robert Hooke, in 1676:

"What Descartes did was a good step. You have added much several ways, and especially in taking the colors of thin plates into philosophical consideration. If I have seen a little further it is by standing on the shoulders of Giants."

Even still, Newton built his quote on the shoulders of a 12th century giant, theologian and author John of Salisbury, who wrote something similar in a treatise on logic called *Metalogicon*, written in Latin in 1159.

"We are like dwarfs sitting on the shoulders of giants. We see more, and things that are more distant, than they did, not because our sight is superior or because we are taller than they, but because they raise us up, and by their great stature add to ours."

It's important to expand our thinking and entertain theories even if they seem contrary to our belief systems, or even outlandish. At the very least, it spurs creative thinking and offers counter arguments and new perspectives.

My suggestion to anyone interested in theories of the Anunnaki as being our extraterrestrial creators is, "do the research yourself." I'm sure that by now there is enough freely available information to help you come to your own conclusions. In doing so, be sure to consider many views; from the most fringe, to the most sterile and academic. Allow yourself the freedom of both creative and critical thinking. Don't stop until you have answered all *your* questions and have filled in all the gaps. Build yourself a framework of historical variables and don't succumb exclusively to the methods of hard science or Reductionism. Interpretation based on critical analysis is an important part of historical research, just as it is in science.

Cartesian style Reductionism is at the heart of modern scientific thinking. This method of understanding says that complex systems can be explained by reducing them to their most basic and fundamental parts. There are many data points that must be in place for Reductionism to work well, a luxury we don't often have when looking at the historical or the archaeological record. While this works to some extent, it is not always the most effective approach when dealing with social sciences or humanities.

In history, all variables are, in a sense, dependent. To isolate one as independent is to alter the nature of historical development. Historical variables are not causal. As a historian, archaeologist, or student of the past, there are only *pieces* of history with which to study. Each variable is a piece of the puzzle as a whole. There is a valid need to generalize based on the variables and their connections to gain a more holistic view of past events.

This is why as a social scientist, I often favor Holism, over Reductionism. I believe that natural systems and their properties should be viewed as wholes, not as collections of parts. I believe that humanity is an extremely complex system whose function cannot be fully understood by its pieces alone. We need creative dot connectors, including Sitchin and others, to help open our minds to possibilities outside of our own intellectual comfort zones. Even Isaac Newton allowed himself the privilege of entertaining theories which science would surely deem superstitious and based in fantasy.

Do I believe in the Sitchin's version of the Anunnaki? If I were limited to Reductionism or semantics I would say no; not in the popular sense. But in a holistic way, I can say that I believe there is some greater truth buried deep within the Sumerian myths, as there is with all cultural material. By studying these myths, this truth can be realized but by limiting ourselves to romantic ideas, semantics, or the word of authority figures, we will forever be vulnerable to the story-telling of anyone with enough charisma to convince us into complacency. So, could there be an alternative to the alternative? Is there another way of interpreting the Anunnaki, apart from extraterrestrial beings, mythological characters, or even gods?

As my research continued, I found myself in a situation that would open my eyes to these *other* ways. I was again, pushed to the edge of reality after coming face to face with those whom today call themselves *The Watchers*. These individuals have an alternative way of interpreting the Sumerian mythos; a way that has been revered, understood, and passed down through the ages by an elite group. This group has been hiding in the shadows, working through others in the same way they believe the Anunnaki work through them. Nevertheless, they are divided amongst themselves, like the legendary planet Tiamat, furiously working to pick up the pieces and make order out of chaos.

THE BATTLE WITHIN

"The human understanding is like a false mirror, which, receiving rays irregularly, distorts and discolors the nature of things by mingling its own nature with it."

—Francis Bacon

The Meeting

"Housekeeping!" a woman's voice insisted.

I opened my eyes to a darkened room.

Housekeeping? What time was it?

"Housekeeping!" she shrilled.

"Just a minute, please!" I managed, jumping out of bed.

As I fumbled around, looking for something to wear, the door began to open. Throwing on a robe, I ran to the door, just as it started to open. I unlatched the top lock and opened the door.

"Sorry. I was still sleeping." I said, but the housekeeper said nothing. She rushed past me, making a beeline into the bathroom.

A deep voice echoed through the corridor, "Dr. Lynn."

I looked to see a man in a black suit standing there.

I felt uneasy. "May I help you?" I asked.

"I have come to take you to your meeting. The car is out front. Please meet me in the lobby in no less than ten minutes."

Ten minutes? Was this the driver or the concierge? Who ordered a car?

"Thank you. I'll be down in a minute!" I feigned.

The housekeeper was still in the bathroom replacing the towels, so I ran to the mini bar and grabbed a bottle of water and started to gulp it down. I was inexplicably thirsty. The hotel room door slammed closed. The housekeeper had left without making the bed. She seemed hyper-focused on the bathroom. There was no time to ponder. I ran over to the bathroom, brushed my teeth, put in my contacts, and hurriedly dressed.

I made it to the lobby just in time to see the suited man speaking with the housekeeper. As I approached, the housekeeper scurried over to her cart and pushed it onto an elevator.

"We've been waiting, Dr. Lynn." The man smiled as he escorted me to the black Town Car that was parked curbside. He opened the door and helped me in.

"Good luck." he snickered.

My eyes felt as though they were on fire, as the car whisked me away. I reached into my bag to get a mirror and noticed that I had forgotten my cell phone.

"Great." I muttered.

Wiping away the remnants of makeup from my compact mirror, I could hardly see a thing, with the exception of my blazing red eyes. They were watering, burning, and aching. I struggled to take my contacts out, as the car hit numerous bumps and pot holes. How was I going to appear to the documentary producer now?

I had taken a late night flight to Los Angeles to meet with a man who said he was interested in filming a documentary about my research. It would be our first meeting, primarily about the logistics of shooting. I checked in to my hotel before dawn, but couldn't really remember anything from the point of check-in, to having been awakened by the housekeeper. Now, my eyes looked like garnets and I could hardly see a thing. I sat back and tried to relax.

"Excuse me? Would you happen to know what time it is?" I asked the driver. He didn't respond. It seemed like we had been driving for quite a while. I used to live in L.A., so I am familiar enough with the geography. My hotel couldn't have been more than 35 minutes from downtown, even in the horrendous L.A. traffic. Seeing through the black tinted windows posed a problem since my eyesight had been so compromised. I felt increasingly trapped.

"Excuse me? Would you be able to tell me where exactly we are going? I didn't get the..."

The automatic privacy window rose up before I could say another word. Now, frustrated, I knocked on the window, but to no avail. I sat back, and decided to wait to see how this would play out.

After what seemed like at least two hours, the car came to an abrupt stop. I could hear the driver get out. I waited for a moment, and decided to open the door.

The door won't open!

The doors were locked from the inside. What in the hell was going on?

Suddenly, the door opens, and a cuff-linked arm reaches in and grabs my jacket. He pulls until he rips a button. I struggle a bit, but only enough to recompose myself once I get out (more like removed) from the vehicle.

"Keep your head down and come with us." said a woman's voice. I felt something go over my head.

A blanket?

My eyes were beginning to clear up. Through the wash of tears, I could see a pale leg marching me forward. The click-clack of our shoes told me we were on marble floors. The lights grew more intense, as I noticed a flash of purple on the woman's leg.

A butterfly tattoo. Could this be the woman at the coffee shop where I met with Bill, the retiree? Impossible. That wouldn't make any sense. It must be a coincidence.

As we kept walking, I could hear the trickle of a water fountain, echoing in the distance. We must have been somewhere large enough to have a fountain. We took the elevator up, or so it felt. Upon reaching our floor, a man told the woman to put me in room 32. I waited as she unlocked the door.

My neck snapped back as I felt a hand push me into the room.

"Make yourself comfortable, Dr. Lynn. You won't be leaving anytime soon." the woman said, as she closed the door.

I pulled the covering from my head and tossed it on a chair. My eyes still a bit watery, I started feeling the walls in an effort to find a light switch. I caught the faint scent of burning wood and noticed a small flicker of light, bouncing off of the shiny wood table.

"I apologize for the trouble, Dr. Lynn. Thank you for seeing me." a man said.

84

"I can hardly see you." I retorted.

"Well, it's probably for the best. We don't really need everyone knowing about this place. Please, sit down."

"I will, as soon as you explain to me what's going on!" I demanded.

"As you've probably guessed, I am not a producer. I didn't mean to mislead you, there. You have to understand; this was the only way I could meet with you and ensure the safety of us both."

The deep creak of the leather chair as I sat at the table sent a chill down my legs. Across the table was a man with icy blue eyes.

"Who are you, and what do you want?" I stammered, trying my best to sound confident.

"I mean you no harm, Dr. Lynn. I simply want to talk. I'm a whistleblower, you see."

I sat up indignantly, "A whistleblower? You strike me as more of a person whom the whistleblowers contact me about!"

"Please, Dr. Lynn. Just wait for a moment before you judge. I thought you were open-minded, or is that just a line you save for the radio?" his tone grew increasingly snide.

"I *am* open-minded, but I don't think anyone would appreciate being misled and ambushed like this. Why am I here? I take it this is not a meeting about a television documentary, is it?" I mocked.

"I guess you're smarter than those boots make you appear!" he laughed.

Why does it always come down to the boots?

"Dr. Lynn, I wanted to speak with you today, because after reading your report about the new archaeological discoveries near Ur, I could tell that you needed some gaps filled in." he offered.

"So you are the person to do that?" I asked. "I don't even know who you are."

"That is probably better for you, in the long run. Let me just say, what I'm about to tell you is something that has been held sacred by my people since the very beginning."

"Your people? Are you a Native American?" I asked.

"No, not at all. When I say 'my people' I mean, my bloodline."

The hairs on the back of my neck stood up. *Am I speaking to someone delusional? What have I gotten myself into?*

Moments like these make me long for a tenure track position at a nice suburban community college somewhere, teaching future nurses and accounting clerks banal facts about the war of 1812.

"You see, my family can trace our lineage to the Sumerian King list. This is how we know that we are entitled to our position, but before I go into all of that, let me start by asking what you know about the Tablet of Destinies."

I knew a fair amount about the Tablet of Destinies, but I did not want to engage any further. I was more interested in what this stranger had to say, and in going home.

"A little, but not that much." I said, playing a bit coy.

Brushing a strand of thick blonde hair from his brow, he smiled and said, "Well, I would be happy to tell you more about it, but I think you know more than you're letting on."

After an awkward pause, he picked up the candle, got up from his chair, and came over. Sitting on the heavy wooden table in front of me, he leaned in and whispered, "I am a Watcher."

His breath on my ear made me tremble. I shifted in my seat.

"Do *you* know what a Watcher is?" he asked, still invading my personal space.

"I know what they were to the ancients." I said.

The man pulled back.

"Then the answer is, yes." he said.

"Do you mean to imply that you are some sort of deity, alien, hybrid, or what?" I suggested.

"We've never gone away. We've only evolved. I wanted to reach out to you because there are a lot of things happening between the families which I don't agree with, a lot of wrong directions being taken. I also want you to tell me if you know where the Tablet of Destinies is. I have reason to believe that you have seen it."

"I don't know how you would think that." I argued. The tall blonde man chuckled and said that this was "why he liked me." He went on to disclose how he and his friends discuss my work, as well as the work of others in the "alternative" fields.

Over the next seven or so hours, he continue to tell me all about his family, what he was raised to believe, and to what religion the so-called Watchers practiced. He offered to fund my excavations, which I declined. I told him that I can't be bought.

He agreed to let me go, as long as I wore a blindfold back to my hotel and traveled with a chaperone. He also made me promise to keep his identity a secret, in exchange for the information he divulged. Like all whistleblowers, regardless of income or status, he should be protected, hence his identity shall remain anonymous.

A Virtual Attack

Shortly after returning to the hotel, I received a call from the front desk asking that I come down to pick up a letter. The only problem was, that no one in L.A. knew what hotel I was staying in, with the exception of the mysterious blonde man.

I picked up the letter. It was hand-written on a blue piece of paper. It only said "You were warned." I got a little creeped out and left that very weekend. When I got back to the east coast, I decided to try to forget the whole thing and move on with my research. A week later, I couldn't get into my email account and everything else started to fall like dominoes.

I discovered that I had been locked out of all of my online accounts. Somehow, my emails, social media, personal, and even bank accounts had been compromised and taken over. It took weeks to get my Facebook page back. I had to start a new account on Instagram, after being told the original one would be investigated and shut down. As I write this, I can still no longer access my Twitter. My website was also attacked, making it so that I could not update my news feed or blog.

In addition to dealing with the virtual takeover of my social media and communication channels, all of my personal accounts, including my bank accounts, had been compromised. As a result, I was thrown into a financial mess. My accounts were frozen pending further investigation. I lost hundreds of dollars and my only recourse was to go through, one by one, to dispute the charges that were made. There I sat; broke and with no communications. I couldn't help but wonder if this had anything to do with the man that I met in Los Angeles.

While I still don't know exactly who was responsible for this attack, they were able to turn my life upside down, if only for a few months. There were moments after which, when I considered giving up my quest. I snapped out of it and realized that to do so would mean they win. I recommitted to my quest, and forged ahead with renewed determination.

This wasn't the first confrontation I had over this book. My initial plan was to publish *Land of the Watchers* much earlier. Before doing so, I was contacted by a law firm claiming to represent parties interested in the contents of my upcoming book. I was told that I needed to submit my manuscript to *them* before publishing or "face harsh consequences." I refused, and was threatened again. I contacted my attorney and he advised that I should simply change some of the names and details in the book so that it could be "inspired by actual events" and then it would be protected from litigation.

Perhaps these were the people behind the letter and attack. Maybe these events aren't even related. This could have all been a random series of coincidences. Still, I increased cyber security and moved ahead with the publishing of this book. On the advice of my attorney, I have changed the names and certain details in this account to protect the innocent. I trust that my readers are smart enough to distinguish fact from fiction.

Nevertheless, I continued my research, only to find out that much of what the blonde man said, turned out to be based in historical truth. It also corroborated some of what the other interviewees reported, including Bill, Derek, and even Professor Shaftner. Ultimately, this would point me back to Ur.

Tablet of Destinies

According to members of the group calling themselves, The Watchers, there is a powerful artifact which they believe can give them the legal authority to rule over Earth. What is this tablet? Where did it come from? Where is it now?

Let's start by looking at one of the first places it's mentioned in the Sumerian texts. It is in an epic poem called, *Ninurta and the Turtle*. The following translation of Ninurta and the Turtle is from Oxford's Electronic Text Corpus of Sumerian Literature, and is used in this context as a means to teach, inform, and spread the knowledge of these important texts. The democratization of ancient wisdom is an important aspect of historiographical scholarship which we must keep as the keynote of our analysis. *Note reader: the following excerpts are exactly as translated and have not been edited for grammar or punctuation. To edit, even for clarity, would introduce unintentional bias by the interpreter.*

Ninurta and the Turtle

(unknown number of lines missing)

Segment A

(8 lines damaged)

(unknown number of lines missing)

Segment B

At his command your weapon struck me evilly. As I let the me go out of my hand, these me returned to the abzu. As I let the divine plan go out of my hand, this divine plan returned to the abzu. This

tablet of destinies returned to the abzu. I was
stripped of the me.'

Ninurta was stunned at these words of the Anzu
chick. Ninmena gave out a wail: 'And what about
me? These me have not fallen into my hand. I
shall not exercise their lordship. I shall not live
(?) like him in the shrine, in the abzu.'
Father Enki in the abzu knew what had been
said.
The chick Anzu took the hero Ninurta by his
hand and drew near with him to Enki's place, the
abzu. The chick Anzu returned Uta-ulu to the
abzu. The lord was delighted with the hero, fa-
ther Enki was delighted with the hero Ninurta.

The lord Nudimmud honoured him duly: 'Hero,
no god among your brother gods could have acted
so. As for the bird which your mighty weapon
captured, from now to eternity you will keep your
foot placed on its neck. May the great gods give
your heroic strength its due. May your father En-
lil do whatever you command. May Ninmena not
fashion your equal (?). May no one be as awesome
as you and no god extend an upraised hand be-
fore you. Monthly may your house (?) regularly re-
ceive tributes in the shrine, in the abzu. May An
(?) proclaim your name in the seat of honour.'

The hero secretly was not happy with these promises. Where he stood, he darkened and yellowed like (?) a flood-storm (?). He contemplated great deeds and inwardly he was rebellious. He uttered a word which has no .... The hero Ninurta set his sights on the whole world. He told no one and inwardly did not ....

The great lord Enki intuitively grasped the substance of the plan. In the shrine, in the abzu he stirred up a dark flood-storm.

By the house the minister Isimud opposed Ninurta. The hero Ninurta refused to come out and raised his hand against the minister Isimud.

Against Ninurta, Enki fashioned a turtle from the clay of the abzu. Against him he stationed the turtle at an opening, at the gate of the abzu. Enki talked to him near the place of the ambush and brought him to the place where the turtle was. The turtle was able to grab Ninurta's tendon from behind. The hero Ninurta managed to turn back its feet. Enki, as if perplexed, said, 'What is this!' He had the turtle scrape the ground with its claws, had it dig an evil pit. The hero Ninurta fell into it with the turtle. The hero did not know how

to get out from .... The turtle kept on gnawing
his feet with its claws (?).

The great lord Enki said to him: 'From ......, you
who set your mind to kill me, ... who makes big
claims - I cut down, I raise up. You who set your
sights on me like this - what has your position
seized for you, how ......? Where has your strength
fled? Where is your heroism? In the great moun-
tains you caused destruction, but how will you get
out now?'

Ninmena learned of this situation. She
ripped the clothes on her body and she .... 'You
my plant-eater Enki, who shall I send to you?
Men will shake their heads in fear .... Who shall
I send to you? That name is not Enki. That name
is Ugugu-that-does-not-pour (?). You who are
death which has no mercy, who shall I send to
you?'

(unknown number of lines missing)

Fig. 5-A: Ninurta with his thunderbolts pursues Anzû
stealing the Tablet of Destinies from Enlil's sanctuary
(Austen Henry Layard Monuments of Nineveh, 2nd Series, 1853)

While no working descriptions of the Tablet or its contents are available, we know from Enuma Elish, Tiamat gives this tablet to Kingu, which puts him in charge of her army of "star-beings, " as some have translated. Then, Marduk goes on to battle Tiamat and her army. Taking the Tablet of Destinies from Kingu's breast, he seals it with his own seal and puts it on. This leads us to believe the Tablet could be worn. In the poem, *Ninurta and the Turtle,* it is Enki, who has possession of the Tablet, which would later be stolen by the bird Anzû (Imdugud).

The bird Anzû, often depicted as half lion and half eagle, is an important and revered symbol to the aristocracy, and has been for thousands of years. It is the Anzû steals the the crown, or umsimi, from the Anunnaki. It is the Anzû that would artistically evolve to become the double-headed eagle, recognizable on heraldry and the symbols of the Scottish Rite of the Freemasons, which we will soon discuss.

Before we look more closely at this symbol, and its relationship to power, let's first tackle the idea that a single tablet could act as a binding law between the gods and man, as this is an important component to understanding not only the history of power and control, but also the future. This Tablet, as well as other decrees, were the original weapons of mass destruction. Their installation brought about the very shift in humanity that turned us from peaceful, spiritual, natural, and egalitarian hunter gathers, to the controlled, oppressed, enslaved, "us versus them," bureaucratic dystopia that we see throughout the historic record.

So often, people ask if the weapons archaeologist are looking for beneath the desert sands in the Middle East are weapons of physical warfare. Are they nuclear weapons? Ancient chemical weapons? Or perhaps something technologically advanced, yet unfamiliar to us in modernity? While I believe there is a great chance that we may one day find amazingly advanced technology, far surpassing what we believe the ancients were capable of, this is not what they are searching for now. Now, they seek to weaponized culture.

Fig. 5-C: Alabaster votive relief of Ur-Nanshe, king of Lagash, showing Anzû as a lion-headed eagle, ca. 2550–2500 BCE.

Fig. 5-D: Anzû with deer. Panel found at the base of the temple of Goddess Ninhursag at Tell- Al-Ubaid. From southern Mesopotamia (Iraq), early dynastic period, circa 2500 BCE. (The British Museum).

WEAPONS OF MASS DESTRUCTION

"All violence consists in some people forcing others, under threat of suffering or death, to do what they do not want to do."

—Leo Tolstoy

The Metaphysics of Control

As we examined in the beginning of the book, Sumerian inventions improved the day to day lives of the ancients and eventually, ours. By contrast, they are the very mechanisms that threaten to destroy it. The invention of complex governmental, financial, and bureaucratic systems which comprise the real *weapon of mass destruction*.

Too often, we think of weapons in a purely physical form, but the weapons of culture are often the most dangerous. By confining the masses to a narrowly defined set of parameters, those interested in maintaining complete control can easily do so. I discuss this in my book, *Anthrotheology* in greater detail, but allow me to elaborate on this point.

As long as humans maintain a corporeal existence, we need some form of worldly order. Laws, institutions, arithmetic, record keeping, speaking; these are all necessities. These are also markers of civilization and what makes the Sumerians, as well as us, different than the earlier hunter gatherer settlements like Göbekli Tepe. However, barriers that limit our expression of free will are weapons of control. These barriers often arise from a power struggle between our will, and the will of opposing forces. If we do not wake up and fight for our freedom, but instead, grow complacent, accepting the barrier around us we can find ourselves in what I refer to as, the *Cycle of Controlled Consciousness*.[13]

In this theory, the duality of man's natural state of mind is what leaves him vulnerable to control. There are two parallel cycles; Corporeal Realm and Spiritual Realm. Both cycles start with Communication. In the Corporeal Realm, the cycle starts with a communication that is specifically described as *ex*pired or, in the Latin tradition, meaning breathed out of. This is the type of conscious energy that influences the Zeitgeist of a culture. They are imposed upon people, rather than individually *in*spired. Through history, we see that the imposed values in the corporeal realm are often materialism, commercialism, consumerism, greed, usury, disregard for life, apathy, etc.

These energies are poured onto the collective, using methods involving the manipulation of symbols, such as in advertising, brands, specific words, emblems, flags, even violence; the most extreme way to communicate negative messages.

Once a source, like a king for example, has communicated their message, it effects the creative force of others and can be recognized in a physical, rather than metaphysical way, for instance, building projects and law making. This is when the symbols are "set in stone." Having now materialized, they have become a shared reality, often becoming the remnants of a lost civilization or the artifacts buried in the archaeological record.

It doesn't take long until the people themselves have used their energy and creativity to create a reality around them, inspired only by what was expired by those at the top. By then, it is too late. Literal and figurative walls have been built and limits have been placed upon everyone's potential, like the walls of an ancient city. The culture is bound by what *appears* to be the natural order. This is why symbolizing abstract ideas in a material way is so important in controlling others.

It adds a sense of realness and serves to keep everyone's consciousness unified and corralled like sheep.

It is at this point, where control is firmly established. This is when organized religion, government, political establishments, and various social hierarchies come into being. They propagate the cycle and reinforce the will of the initiator, or king, in this example

In order to have complete control over his newly created kingdom, a king would need subjects whose only function would have been serving at his will. Since the subjects' innate creative forces were co-opted, they would have not had enough energy to devote to making their own world. This exhaustion and inefficacy led to dependency on the king and his world, and the safety of the walled in city. This dependency consequently led to fear of banishment from the kingdom. Self-sufficiency was too overwhelming by that point. So, it was much easier for the king to build control systems around them, sealing their fate as "trapped" sheep. This is why many of the themes of ancient mythology center on the struggle between nature and civility, just as in the traditional interpretation of the Epic of Gilgamesh.

Once control has been accomplished, the cycle begins again. Now, the members of the society

104

start to subjugate themselves. They do this by repeating the will of the king, socially ostracizing those who may seek to create a world for themselves that differs from the accepted narrative.

Not much has changed in modernity. This model can even be applied on a much more individualized scale. Have you ever felt trapped by society's expectations? Have you ever wondered why you are supposed to look like ___, act like___, be like___, feel like___? Have you ever felt so tired of the "rat race" that you have no time to pursue your own passions and dreams? Do you sometimes lack inspiration? Do you feel that you have been given a particular lot in life and you can't do much to change it? This, is the Cycle of Controlled Consciousness in the Corporeal Realm.

In the Spiritual Realm, the cycle can be recognized a bit differently. Transmission of a wholly inspired message is communicated through the creation of art, poetry, music, etc. This is something many artists experience while they are creating. Meditation can help to facilitate the "breathing in" or inspiration of messages. To be whole, we must open ourselves to creative inspiration, and not expire through conditioned mass consumption.

When the energy behind this inspiration is communicated, it can inspire others to create in a community of cooperation. The results generally benefit the entire culture, rather than one king. The people are not subjugated, rather, they are co-existing in a consciously created reality which they have willingly created.

The creative force thrives, allowing abundance and prosperity. The control aspect of the Cycle of Controlled Consciousness of the Spiritual Realm is *self*-control. By relinquishing control of others (a control often impossible to maintain) and mastering your own perception, you will no longer feel exhausted. Rather, you will feel invigorated and ready to share your good will with everyone. You will be the liberator, rather than the subjugator.

When body/mind synthesis is fully achieved, man will break from the Cycle of Controlled Consciousness and move in an upward trajectory towards higher consciousness. This synthesis between what is external and what is internal, I believe, is the true meaning of ascension, sometimes referred to as Christ-consciousness. It is a fate which is available to us all if we choose to accept it.

The fact that we, as a people, are trapped in this cycle is a testament to the great shift in world order that happened during the time of the Sumerians. This world order, forever changed the way life was lived on this planet. In the *Enuma Elish*, the creation of the universe is explained. In *Ninurta and the Turtle*, the shift in power is outlined. However, in *Enki and the World Order,* a form, function and purpose is created on the planet Earth. The corporeal realm was formed, building the walls of both stone and culture. Enki, the lord of the Earth, is described as a "craftsman." These descriptions have led some to associate Enki with Lucifer. Again, the following excerpts are exactly as translated by Samuel Noah Kramer, in his text, *The Sumerians, Their History, Culture and Character* (Chicago: University of Chicago Press, 1963, and have not been edited for grammar or punctuation. To edit, even for clarity, would introduce unintentional bias by the interpreter.

Enki and the World Order

Enki, the king of the Abzu, overpowering in his
majesty, speaks up with authority:
'My father, the king of the universe,
Brought me into existence in the universe,
My ancestor, the king of all the lands,
Gathered together all the, me's, placed the me's in
my hand.
From the Ekur, the house of Enlil,
I brought craftsmanship to my Abzu of Eridu.
I am the fecund seed, engendered by the great
wild ox, I am the f irst born son of An,
I am the "great storm" who goes forth out of the
"great below," I am the lord of the Land,
I am the gugal of the chieftains, I am the father of
all the lands,
I am the "big brother" of the gods, I am he who
brings full prosperity,
I am the record keeper of heaven and earth,
I am the car and the mind of all the lands,
I am he who directs justice with the king An on
An's dais,
I am he who decrees the fates with Enlil in the
"mountain of wisdom," He placed in my hand the
decreeing of the fates of the "place where the sun
rises,"
I am he to whom Nintu pays due homage,

I am he who has been called a good name by Nin-
hursag,

I am the leader of the Anunnaki,
I am he who has been born as the first son of the
holy An.
After the lord had uttered (his) exaltedness,
After the great Prince had himself pronounced his
praise,
The Anunnaki came before him in prayer and
supplication:
'Lord who directs craftsmanship,
Who makes decisions, the glorified; Enki praise!'
For a second time, because of his great joy,:
Enki, the king of the Abzu, in his majesty, speaks
up with authority
'I am the lord, I am one whose command is un-
questioned, I am the
foremost in all things,
At my command the stalls have been built, the
sheepfolds have been
enclosed,
When I approached heaven a rain of prosperity
poured down from
heaven,
When I approached the earth, there was a high
flood,
When I approached its green meadows,

The heaps and mounds were piled up at my word.
[After the almost unintelligible description of En-
ki's rites, Enki proceeds
to decree the fates of a number of cities. Ur is one
example.]
He proceeded to the shrine Ur,
Enki, the ki-ng of the Abzu decrees its fate:
City possessing all that is appropriate, water-
washed, ftrm-standing ox,
Dais of abundance of the highland, knees open,
green like a mountain,
Hashur-grove, wide of shade-he who is lordly be-
cause of his might
Has directed your perfect mes,
Enlil, the "great mountain," has pronounced your
lofty -name in the universe.
City whose fate has been decreed by Enlil,
Shrine Ur, may you rise heaven high
[Enki next stocks the land with various items of
prosperity: A deity
is placed in charge of each. For example:]
He directed the plow and the . . . yoke,
The great prince Enki put the 'horned oxen' in the
. . . Opened the holy furrows,
Made grow the grain in the cultivated field.
The lord who do-ns the diadem, the ornament of
the high plain, The robust,,the farmer of Enlil,

110

*Enkimdu, the man of the ditch and dike, Enki
placed in charge of them.
The lord called the cultivated field, put there the
checkered grain, Heaped up its . . . grain, the
checkered grain, the innuba-grain into piles,
Enki multiplied the heaps and mounds,
With Enlil he spread wide the abundance in the
Land,
Her whose head and side are dappled, whose face
is honey-covered, The Lady, the procreatress, the
vigour of the Land, the 'life' of the black-heads,
Ashnan, the nourishing bread, the bread of all,
Enki placed in charge of them.
He built stalls, directed the purification rites,
Erected sheepfolds, put there the best fat and
milk,
Brought joy to the dining halls of the gods,
In the vegetation-like plain he made prosperity
prevail.*

....

*He filled the Ehur, the house of Enlil, with pos-
sessions,
Enlil rejoiced with Enki, Nippur was joyous,
He fixed the borders, demarcated them with
boundary stones,
Enki, for the Anunnaki,
Erected dwelling places in the cities,*

111

Set up kids for them in the countryside,
The hero, the bull who comes forth out of the
hashur (forest), who roars lion-like,
The valiant Utu, the bull who stands secure, who
proudly displays his power,
The father of the great city, the place where the
sun rises, the great herald of holy An,
The judge, the decision-maker of the gods,
Who wears a lapis lazuli beard, who comes forth
from the holy heaven,
the ... heaven,
Utu, the son born of Ningal,
Enki placed in charge of the entire universe.

In this tablet, there is an important line, in reference to Enki: "*Has directed your perfect mes.*" The mes were official decrees of the gods that were the foundations to all attributes of a higher civilization. A me was a law, or set of holy instructions which guided technologies, religious and ceremonial practices, etiquette, social institution. Think of these as legally binding cultural blueprints. Me(s), as in the word Mesopotamia, which means "between two rivers" literally meant *between*. Thus, these doctrines were binding because they came straight from the gods themselves. They were the first covenants.

Originally, mes were collected by Enlil, the spirit, then given to Enki, lord of the earthly realm, who could materialize them. Enki would then broker the mes to the selected rulers at Sumerian administrative centers, starting with the city of Eridu, and on to Ur, as *Enki and the World Order* details.

Just as with the Tablet of Destinies, there are no specific physical descriptions of these mes. We do know, however, that in one tablet, the goddess Inanna displays them to the people of Uruk, upon her arrival in "the boat of heaven." In this account, the mes are not only represented as tablets, but also functional tools and artifacts, such as musical instruments.

113

Just when the myths have us thinking we know what these mes are, we come to find that not all of them were actually tangible. Some, were conceptual. How these mes were displayed is still a mystery. Not only were they conceptual or abstract, some were also negative. Some of these mes would come to represent all that is evil and destructive in humanity.

So, these Sumerian gods dictated and instructed the first kings, whom were installed at these city centers to "destroy other cities." They encouraged "falsehood," yet taught the functions of "victory," as heroism. Thus, evil and sin were divinely decreed, and royally enforced.

Enki appeared in the physical realm, so he needed a medium to channel the other gods. To communicate with the others, he would sometimes summon the bird Anzû (Imdugud), as his messanger.

"The prince calls his messenger Imdugud,
Enki gives the word to the 'good name of heaven':
'Oh my messenger Imdugud, 'my good name of
heaven'.'
'Oh my king Enki, here I stand, forever is praise.'
'The boat of heaven, where now has it arrived?'"

According to the account given by Samuel Noah Kramer, in his important work, *The Sumerians: Their History, Culture, and Character*, over one hundred separate mes appear on tablet fragments. They include:

- Enship (meaning a type of stewardship over human beings)
- Godship
- The exalted and enduring crown
- The throne of kingship
- The exalted sceptre
- The royal insignia
- The exalted shrine
- Shepherdship
- Kingship
- Lasting ladyship
- "Divine lady" (a priestly office)
- Ishib (a priestly office)
- Lumah (a priestly office)
- Guda (a priestly office)
- Truth
- Descent into the nether world
- Ascent from the nether world
- Kurgarra (a eunuch, or, possibly, ancient equivalent to modern concepts of androgyne or transsexual [6])
- Girbadara (a eunuch)

- Sagursag (a eunuch, entertainers related to the cult of Inanna [?])
- The battle-standard
- The flood
- Weapons
- Sexual intercourse
- Prostitution
- Law
- Libel
- Art
- "hierodule of heaven"
- Music
- Eldership
- Heroship
- Power
- Enmity
- Straightforwardness
- The destruction of cities
- Lamentation
- Rejoicing of the heart
- Falsehood
- Art of metalworking
- Scribeship
- Craft of the smith
- Craft of the leatherworker
- Craft of the builder
- Craft of the basket weaver
- Wisdom

- Attention
- Holy purification
- Fear
- Terror
- Strife
- Peace
- Weariness
- Victory
- Counsel
- The troubled heart
- Judgment
- Decision
- Lilis (a musical instrument)
- Ub (a musical instrument)
- Mesi (a musical instrument)
- Ala (a musical instrument)
- Guslim (a musical instrument)

These mes, are important to our understanding of human development, and the role the Sumerians played. This is the first time in history we see such a highly advanced system of rule in place; a system that was divinely decreed. They were inspired (through the spirit came) by Enil, which possessed Enki to take action here on Earth. Enki was the earthly, biological mediator. Though the Sumerian accounts have him eating, drinking, and colluding with humans in the Earthly plane, he held his position still higher than those he called "the black headed ones," or humans. He was their lord. To maintain this balance of power, Enki lived high in the mountains, and had gatekeepers. These were the world's first human kings, and their bloodlines were carefully recorded. Evidence of this can be traced to the Sumerian King List.

In this tradition, kingship was handed down directly by the gods. If the human king moved to another city, his kingship would be transferred from one city to another, which gave the perception of intrinsic authority. No one would necessarily question this perceived authority. This divided people, making the original 99% against 1%.

This 1%, the select few kings of Enki, ruled over cities and people. Through generations, this closed group, whom carefully guarded their lineage, developed their own parallel set of cultural symbols and practices. These symbols can be traced from the Sumerians, to the ruling elites of today. The most ancient and, to some extent, most important, is that of the bird, Anzû.

Depictions of Anzû can be traced back thousands of years. This double headed bird dates as far back as 3800 B.C.E., and was the Sumerian symbol for Ninurta, the god of Lagash, who would slay Anzû in a fight for the Tablet of Destinies.

Some Biblical scholars believe that this is the original personification of Nimrod.

An interesting and telling depiction of Anzû is on a silver and copper vase dedicated by Entemena, king of Lagash, to Ninurta from 2400 B.C.E. The vase shows Enlil bringing down an "extract" from the constellation Leo to create Ninurta and Entemena both depicted as lions. This is an important cosmology to keep in mind, as it goes back to the first chapter and the importance of the constellation of Leo.

Fig. 6-A: Sumerian King List, the Weld-Blundell prism in the Ashmolean Museum. (1763-1753 B.C.E.)

Fig. 6-B: Entemena's vase. (approx.. 2400 B.C.E.)

The astronomical alignments of Leo, Taurus, and Sirius were very important to the Sumerians, particularly the elites. So, depicted on this vase, we have the two sons of Enki, symbolized as, and created from "extracts" of the constellation Leo. What you'll see next is that the same process was used in the creation of the third brother king, Gudea, who was born under the sign of Taurus. Gudea was called the "architect" of the House of Ningirsu.

There are many statues of Gudea, many of which were made from rare diorite. However, the oldest ever known Gudea's statue, the oldest ever statue of a known king from Mesopotamia, was stolen from the Iraqi Museum. Clearly, this and artifacts like it are of great interest to looters.

These symbols have been important to the elites since the beginning of human *civilization*. They continue to be revered, coveted, and used as a means of communicating their message of authority over humanity to this very day.

According to my sources, this is why elites seek out these artifacts; as trophies. They share the feeling that these symbols rightfully belong to them and should be in *their* possession only. They have a sense of entitlement because they believe they can trace their lineage to the very first kings of Sumer, making them part of the original ruling class.

Symbol of the Ages

The double-headed eagle comes directly from the myth of the Anzû. Having its roots in Sumer, it can also be found in Anatolia, and later Babylon. In fact, examples of this symbol are found all around the world. Over a period of about a thousand years, this symbol spread throughout Asia, India, and Europe.

Scottish Rite Freemasons, new Lagash was an important and powerful city. The god of the city, Ninurta would later become known as Nimrod, a name which is from the Hebrew marad meaning "to rebel." Initially, this god was associated with a single-headed Anzû bird.

Ninurta (Nimrod) had attributes that the Scottish Rite wanted to be aligned with. He was ambitious, confident, and anarchist in nature. This was exemplified in *Ninurta and the Turtle*, when he was willing to rebel against Enki. Ninurta's role as the builder of civilization has been argued as paralleling the Biblical account of Nimrod's building of ancient cities, particularly that of Babylon.

The cult of Ninurta developed as the new center of worship, as the worship of Anu, Enlil, and Enki, moved northwest from Sumer in the third millennium B.C.E. (yet another example of syncretism). Thus, Ninurta, became Nimrod, the builder of the tower of Babel. Remember, it was Nimrod who rebelled against God by building the Tower, much like Ninurta's rebellion.

Many are familiar with the Freemason's reverence for King Solomon. However, in the 15th and 16th centuries, it was Nimrod, not Solomon, who was touted as being the first Freemason. This connected the origins of Masonry to the Tower of Babel, rather than the Temple of Jerusalem.

To many in Abrahamic traditions, Nimrod is the original founder of a one-world totalitarian government; a New World Order. He was the great unifier and master builder. Knowing this, the Scottish rite uses Ninurta's symbol to represent its 32nd and 33rd degrees. Moving forward, this symbol would be used on everything from family crests, such as the Rothschild's, military, government, royalty, large global corporations, and even in the Third Reich. The eagle, known for its superior eyesight, can see in both directions when it has two heads. Hence forth, this creature was associated with the all seeing eye of the elite bloodlines that were sanctioned by the Anunnaki gods to rule over and enslave humanity.

This desire to unify the world under a totalitarian regime, has been bubbling under the surface like an oil seep, throughout all of history since the days of the Sumerian Kings. Which brings us to the question, why would oil companies have an interest in these excavations? Are they, too, looking for the Tablet of Destinies?

Fig. 6-C: Ninurta and the double-headed eagle.

Fig. 6-D: Chrysoboullon of Alexius III of Trebizond (1338-1390). Notice the robe on the right. The pattern is that of the double-headed eagle.

126

Fig. 6-E: Emperor Maximilian with the Imperial Banner (Albrecht Altdorfer, ca. 1515).

Sumerian Mountain Oil

In my research, I have found an interconnected web of facts leading, perhaps unsurprisingly, to oil. While it may come as no big revelation, America's war in the Middle East has been over oil, as have both world wars. The quest for oil has been the cause of innumerable deaths around the world for years and this quest is not new. Many are surprised to learn how ancient humanity's knowledge of oil is. The Sumerian, Akkadians, and Babylonians were aware of the importance of oil, as were Native Americans. Let's take a quick look at ancient oil, starting with the Sumerians.

To start, the term oil is usually used as a more generalized term referring to a viscous flammable liquid, insoluble in water. However, petroleum is a more specific term referring to a hydrocarbon oil found in the upper strata of the earth, which goes through a refining process to be used as fuel. The word petroleum literally means "rock oil," translated from Greek to the Latin *petra* 'rock' and *oleum* 'oil.'

Oil does not always need to be drilled. It can also be found in what are called seeps, or oil springs. When the oil from these springs evaporates, it leaves behind a semi-solid hydrocarbon product called bitumen. This has been used for thousands of years as a waterproofing agent, for plumbing, boat building and brick bonding. It is credited as being the literal glue that held together the Tower of Babel. Petroleum was essential to the infrastructure of Babylon the Great. It was also an important component to ritual sacrifice.

Fig. 6-F: Petroleum seep near the Korňa in northern Slovakia.

Vegetable and animal oils have traditionally been used in Abrahamic religious ceremonies. In fact, the word Christ is from the Latin 'Christus,' which is from Greek 'khristos' meaning "the anointed." This anointing refers to a ceremonial process where oil is smeared on the head. Many are familiar with these etymologies as well as the anointing ceremonies which are still performed in numerous modern religious settings. However, the act of anointing with oil predates the Abrahamic religions. It even predates Egyptian religions, which also anointed with natural oils.

In the Sumerian records, there are many mentions of oils and their uses. Cedar oils, vegetable oils, even bitumen were regularly referenced. However, there is one very special oil that was used in an important ritual. It translates simply to "mountain oil." Could this "mountain oil" be "rock oil" or petroleum?

Mountain oil was thought to have healing and life extension abilities. Those anointed with this particular oil, would have eternal life and favor with the gods. Remember, this was a naturally occurring oil, found only deep within the mountains where the gods resided. It was not the same refined petrol we put into our automobiles today. This was such a special oil, that the only humans allowed to be anointed in this manner, were the kings. Could this be why in the Sumerian King List, the kings' reigns are so unnaturally long?

Once anointed, or christened, these kings would have reached apotheosis, allowing them to ascend to a god status, making them the ultimate Anunnaki server *and* world ruler. It is easy to see why people in positions of power would want to get their hands on this special type of oil.

I have traced this particular mountain oil to the Zagros Mountain range, homeland of Enil, Inanna, and other key figures in Sumerian mythology. This oil was used in a strange, yet familiar, ritual to honor Inanna, the daughter of Nanna and Ningal, who is also associated with Venus, Ishtar, and subsequent fertility goddess symbolism. Nanna, her father, son of Enlil and Ninlil, later became identified with Assyrian moon god Su'en/Sîn, whose name meant "illuminator." His worship center was Ur, whose name literally meant the dwelling place of Nanna. The oil from the mountain home of the Sumerian creator gods was important to Sumerian religious rituals and civil structure.

The Zagros Mountains were a special place. In addition to being the dwelling place and retreat of the Sumerian gods, they were also the home to the first known dragon, named Kur. Kur, the serpent, is so much associated with the mountains, that it is depicted as a picture of a mountain in cuneiform.

Archaeological evidence has revealed interesting clues to the myths of the Zargos Mountain dweller. Serpent-man hybrid clay figurines, excavated by Woolley, have been associated with the Ubaid peoples, who originally came down from the Zagros Mountains of Kurdistan, hence the 'Kur' in Kurdistan (stan = place of or home). So, in addition to the Zargos Mountains being associated with the Sumerian gods, they are also known as housing a great serpent or, in some accounts and translations, serpents. To this day, there are people who believe the ethnic group, Kurds, are serpent people, or reptilians, because of this linguistic connection to Kur, the dragon.

Cuneiform symbol for Kur and Mountain.

Fig. 6-G: Clay serpent man. Ubaid-period.
(6500 to 3800 BCE).

The importance of this mountain range to the modern oil industry cannot be stressed enough. Iran's main oilfields are located on the western central foothills of the Zagros mountain range. Oil is an essential economic power, it was one of the first advanced technologies to revolutionize production, warfare, and society. Big oil, to which it is rightfully referred, is one of the world's largest and most powerful industries. It has colluded with governments, global banks, and elite families since the beginning. However, in the early 1870s, John D. Rockefeller acted as a sort of Nimrod, in that he wanted to unify the oil industry under his authority; he wanted to create a monopoly.

His company, Standard Oil, would eventually control almost 95% of U.S. oil production and refining. Through ruthlessness, intimidation, bribery, and destruction, the Rockefeller family amassed a huge fortune and even political influence that persists to this day.

The U.S. Industrial Revolution wasn't where it ended. In 1928, British, Dutch, and U.S. oil companies divided the Middle Eastern oil market in an effort to fix prices. This led to their intimate involvement in Middle East politics. After World War II, the U.S. Congress, Justice Department, and Federal Trade Commission investigated these arrangements and tried to bring about civil and criminal antitrust charges against the oil companies. However, President Eisenhower wanted to use the oil industry to push the Soviets from Iran, usurping any antitrust concerns. These oil motivated proxy wars continue to this very day.

It isn't only the oil industry with an interest in the region. It is mining and other natural resources, as well. Again, not for the apparent reasons of acquiring raw materials.

I have spent countless hours combing over Sumerian records, searching for clues to human origins and a better understanding of the power structures that have come to dominate our world. In my personal study of the Sumerian tablets, I have found more to support that the Sumerian god's were interested in this mountain oil more than even gold, due to its life extension capabilities.

I was contacted by a university trained economist. After working for a rare metals company in Germany, he wanted to discuss his belief that Sitchin was on to something about how the gods created humans to mine for gold. He said that he believed that humans were not enslaved or forced to mine gold for these gods. Rather, they knew the Anunnaki wanted the gold, so in exchange for mining, they received knowledge of technology, starting with oil. Since this was the first deal humans made with the gods, the gods required the sacrificial burning of oil, even to this day, as a covenant of this arrangement. He went on to state that this is why money is no longer backed by gold, but wealth is mostly determined by oil production. Burning oil, is a symbolic ritual used to invoke the spirit of illumination (Enki).

Some seeking knowledge in advanced technology, do this as a way to symbolize their quest for knowledge. In art through the ages, you will see illumination, knowledge, and education symbolized by a torch or lamp. Oil represents the fuel burned in exchange for illumination. The oil, itself, is the burnt offering.

While this arrangement started slowly, technologies allowed us to mine gold faster. It was the first gold rush. This was, in the economist's words, "why the alchemists wanted to make gold." Gold would allow the person to have ultimate control over this arrangement with the gods. He asked me to consider the value of gold, asking, "Does gold only have value because it's rare?" and that there were "certainly rarer minerals than gold." He claimed that in his job, he needed security clearance to learn about the actual economics of the metal trade. It was then he learned that this early system turned early into a transactional, currency based system.

With all of these ideas, connections, testimonies, and historiographical points, what could this all mean to us now? What are behind current industrial and aristocratic funded archaeological excavations in the Middle East? What about in other places around the world? In this complex and competitive geopolitical landscape, how are we to begin to understand the motives behind looting on such a grand scale?

THE END GAME

"All the sons of men shall not perish in consequence of every secret, by which the Watchers have destroyed, and which they have taught, their offspring."

—Enoch 10:11

Owning the Past

"I certainly did not know that you could actually buy museum quality antiquities!" said Baron Lorne Thyssen, in an interview with Apollo Magazine, May 11, 2014. The wealthy donor to the new excavations near Ur is a notorious collector of ancient art, and heir to one of the richest families in the world. The Thyssen family owns the world's largest and most valuable private collection of ancient relics rivaled only by that of Queen Elizabeth.

If it weren't enough for Baron Lorne Thyssen to amass a huge private collection, he is now in the business of selling these artifacts. He opened a retail front in London devoted to selling Greek antiquities. I'm sure you are wondering how this is even legal. When you are part of the 1%, it appears you are above the law.

Perhaps it is his lineage which gives him this sense of entitlement. The Thyssens are one of the elite bloodlines who may actually believe they can trace their lineage to ancient Mesopotamia. Thyssen family members have made their home in various countries and spread in a corporate imperialist fashion, much like the Rothschild banking family. The Thyssen family has many notable members, all of whom descend from Friedrich Thyssen, who established steel works, elevators, escalators, industrial conglomerates, banks, and massive art collections.

Fritz Thyssen was especially corrupt. He was arrested for refusing to accede to the demands of French authorities occupying the Ruhr. In 1921, the German government charged him with betraying the Ruhr district to the French during the war. It was Fritz who funded the newly formed Nazi party by giving them a large injection of funds ($25,000) in the mid-1920's. In 1931, Fritz Thyssen joined the Nazi Party, and soon became close friends with Adolf Hitler. He continued to use his offshore banks to pump money into the Nazi war machine.

Over the years, Thyssen came to be known as "Hitler's most important and prominent financier". When asked about Hitler, Thyssen was actually quoted as saying, "I realized his orator gifts and his ability to lead the masses. What impressed me most, however, was the order that reigned over his meetings, the almost military discipline of his followers." Thyssen also persuaded the Association of German Industrialists to donate 3 million Reichsmarks to the Nazi Party for the 1933 Reichstag election. As a payback, he was in turn elected a Nazi member of the Reichstag and appointed to the Prussian State Council, the largest German state.

After WWII, Thyssen was tried for being a Nazi supporter, which he did not deny, admitting his support for the exclusion of Jews from German business and mistreatment of his own Jewish employees in the 1930s. As I detail in *The Sumerian Controversy*, Prescott Sheldon Bush (Member of "The Order" 1917), father of George Herbert Walker Bush, was the business partner of Fritz Thyssen. Big oil, big banks, fraternal orders; they all have a place in this story. Yet, the question remains; why are they really funding archaeological excavations?

Project Destiny

As I write this, over a year has passed since I started collecting testimonies and conducting research. One evening, while sitting at my desk, staring at the soft green glow of my banker's lamp, I recalled the meeting with the mysterious blonde man. I remember him going on about a supposed government program he called, *Project Destiny*.

It didn't really stand out to me much at the time, but after putting the pieces together, I think that this what Derek eluded to in our meeting. I also think that perhaps in some strange way, so was Professor Shaftner. The blonde man said, that heads of competing families were trying to find the missing fragments of the Tablet of Destinies. If this were true, what were they hoping to accomplish?

According to the legend, whomever possessed the Tablet of Destinies would have the Divine right of Kings. This would allow them to be the ruler of the universe, but that's not all. The Tablet also granted the power of all past, present, and future knowledge. With this tablet, anyone can be a Watcher, for they would have the ability to "see" in all directions, just like the symbolic double headed eagle.

Fiction reveals truth which reality often obscures. In his 2013 science fiction novel, *The Transhumanist Wager*, atheist transhumanist, Zoltan Istvan outlines the Three Laws of Transhumanism, which are widely studied in intellectual transhumanist circles. These are:

1. A transhumanist must safeguard one's own existence above all else.

2. A transhumanist must strive to achieve omnipotence as expediently as possible— so long as one's actions do not conflict with the First Law.

3. A transhumanist must safeguard value in the universe—so long as one's actions do not conflict with the First and Second Laws.

The transhumanist agenda can be clearly identified in the alleged *Project Destiny*. Some mega wealthy elite, like Ray Kurzweil, director of engineering at Google, predicts that humans will become hybrids with artificial remote intelligence in the 2030s. While speaking at the Exponential Finance conference in New York, he said, "We're going to gradually merge and enhance ourselves," meaning that our brains will be able to connect directly to a system of computers in the cloud, via nanobots, tiny robots made from DNA strands. He goes on to lament, "In my view, that's the nature of being human -- we transcend our limitations."

Transhumanism is not new. Man's quest to become god is thousands of years old, as evident in the Sumerian myths we've examined in this book. This quest for the "fountain of youth" will undoubtedly go on in perpetuity, or at least as long as humans are mortal. When man becomes wealthy beyond compare, when he accumulates as much worldly knowledge as his gray matter will accept, when he is revered, or in some cases feared, by the masses, he is by most accounts, lord of this world. Nevertheless, his fate is sealed in his humanity. All of these worldly treasures mean nothing to him, once he is gone. Throughout all of human history, the only power past the grave great men have had is legend. This is why there is an arcane fetish for the notion of "hero."

Hero Complex

What exactly is a hero in a historical and cultural context? To the Greeks, heroes were men who once lived, but were so great their legacy remained a source of national pride. Epics such as *The Aeneid* and *The Odyssey* use story and imagination to tell history and engage the masses in a sense of cultural connectivity. Authors such as Virgil and Homer wished for a connection to be made between their stories and the greater truths of the human condition. As Virgil said, *"Sunt lacrimae rerum et mentem mortalia tangent"* or, "Here are tears for man's adversities and mortal affairs touch the heart." It is the important difference between a mere report of events and a myth and why both of these stories have endured.

Arguably one of the most important epic poems, *The Aeneid*, is a well-known example of such a myth. Written between 30 B.C.E. and 19 B.C.E., by Roman poet Publius Vergilius Maro, more commonly known as Virgil, *The Aeneid* consists of 12 books in dactylic hexameter verse. The story is centered on the life of Aeneas, who flees the city of Troy during its sacking, with his son, Ascanius and his father, Anchises. Aeneas is guided by prophetic wisdom to Italy, believing that he will have a future kingdom there. According to Virgil, his descendants make up the Roman people. The Aeneid was so influential to the culture of ancient Rome, it established Aeneas as a hero and a new icon of Roman virtue.

Similarly, *The Odyssey*, was an influential epic poem which served as a history for the ancient Greek people. Estimated to have been written in approximately 800 B.C.E. by Greek poet Homer, *The Odyssey* is divided into 24 books and is in dactylic hexameter verse. Much like *The Aeneid, The Odyssey* deals with aftermath of the Trojan War. The main character is named Odysseus. Odysseus has been away from his home in Ithaca for almost twenty years. While away at war in Troy, a bevy of suitors try to take his wife, Penelope. Their interest is not in Penelope as a partner; so much as it is in what she has. Whoever marries Penelope will be able to claim Odysseus' kingdom. Penelope however is able to hold off suitors while she waits steadfastly for Odysseus to come back to her, which, spoiler alert, he eventually does.

The main characters also have a similar demeanor that is different than stories' supporting characters. Odysseus is more of a contemplative hero who is not as quick to act. This is similar to Aeneas, who is also more contemplative. Both Odysseus and Aeneas struggle to understand their place in the world and what, if any, control they may have over their lives in light of the influence of unpredictable gods. This reflects common sentiments not only in the lives of the people in the ancient Greco-Roman world, but also the Sumerians, and arguably, ours.

As is the case with most heroes, the character of Aeneas is a carefully contrived version of a man, put forth to represent the ideal man of the culture for which it was written. This is a hero who could be raised to a cult status for his ability to embody the virtues most valued by the ancient Romans of Virgil's time. Not unlike Aeneas, Odysseus also served as a hero, providing a similar sense of cultural cohesion for the ancient Greek people. For example, he was able to overcome extreme dangers of both adversaries and creatures on his journey. He also represented virtue because of his loyalty to his family. During his almost twenty years away from home, he is comforted only by the thoughts of his wife and son. By character, he is intelligent and able to get out of potential defeating situations by using his wit. He is also portrayed as the man who was responsible for saving the Greeks in the Trojan War, helping them to win, as it was his idea to make the Trojan Horse. This use of disguise and trickery is very characteristic of Odysseus. From all perspectives, Odysseus is a winner. After a dangerous and daunting journey, he doesn't lose faith and ends up reuniting with his family and in good graces with the gods. All of these enabled the Greek people to view

Odysseus as a hero; an idealized version of the Greek man.

While different, these two epic poems depict the idealized hero, the notions of which sprung from the cultural pressures of their respective geographies and times. Virgil and Homer gave their audiences a more relatable experience of the hero by bringing it to a level which they could relate and understand. The sentiments expressed in each are all part of the human experience. Although fiction, both *The Aeneid* and *The* Odyssey appeal to emotion and desire to feel connected to a common ancestry. This sense of national pride and cultural identification creates social cohesion, something vitally important to both ancient Rome and ancient Greece, as they were both comprised of smaller, multicultural groups within one growing system. It was imperative in both societies to unite the people under the banner of a common history, one worthy of pride.

Mythic heroes have been immortalized through poetry, art, music, and myth because they offered not only a connection to the past, but also a connection between the natural and supernatural worlds. These captivating and enduring works have shaped how people in the ancient Greco-Roman world identified themselves and subsequently, the egos and aspirations of the political ruling class. Meanwhile, the sheeple are busy idolizing celebrity and espousing virtues only conducive to economic gain for the elites.

These were the ways of the Old World Order, when all a great man could do to maintain power and influence, even after death, was become a hero in the classical sense. His legacy was all he had. In modernity, man has ever evolving technologies which could soon lead him to what the Greco-Romans could have only imagined; immortality.

Making the Connection

After publishing my initial report and having the opportunity to meet so many people with diverse points of view, I was no longer surprised when contacted by people wanting to share their thoughts. What was surprising, however, was the wide variety of people who contacted me. In addition to U.F.O. researchers such as Bill, military veterans like Derek, I was contacted by a number of industry insiders, globalist, bankers, and members of elite families. Not one person, with the exception of the attorney I spoke of earlier, had anything negative to say. In fact, most wrote to me, stating that they enjoyed my work and found it fascinating. Some, wanted to keep in touch.

Now, I wasn't sure what to make of this. Was this a case of "Keep your enemies close?" My intention is never to make enemies. My intention is to bring to light new ways of looking at some of these issues. With so many of these people contacting me, I am left to wonder; what are the true beliefs held by those in the most powerful positions in the world?

We have all maybe met a man like Bill, the retiree. Some would look at Bill as simply "tin foil hat wearer." Why are his beliefs not taken seriously? I think it is because they rattle the minds of people who are afraid to think freely. I also think social status play a significant role. People with little relative means and very imaginative ways of seeing or believing are usually called crazy. However, you may have the same ways of seeing and believing, but if you have a higher social status, you may simply be called eccentric. In some cases, you may even be seen as a forward thinking intellectual or futurist!

Who Cares?

So again, why should we care what big oil, mining, and energy corporations, aristocratic families, and a host of other nefarious groups do in the desert in another country? Because the more we ignore the problems of this world, the less will ever change.

Archaeology is an important tool of influence. If this were not the case, ISIS wouldn't be destroying ancient World Heritage sites and killing scholars. Archaeological discoveries are sources of national pride and have the power to unify populations. Remember, if you systematically erase the past, you can control the future by filling in the blanks with whatever you want people to believe. This is the weaponization of history, my friends.

Corporate elites are routinely purchasing and stealing the cultural heritage of vulnerable populations. Don't be fooled if these artifacts end up in exhibits. The scholars who are allowed to examine these artifacts are a select few from a network of cronies. They are hand-picked. Remember the picture of the Hall of Human Origins, in the Smithsonian museum. The Hall is funded by one of the infamous Koch Brothers. Philanthropy is often only strategic public relations, in order to receive good press, thereby burying the bad. It's a trick perfected, if not originated, by the Rockefellers and other oligarchs of the Industrial Revolution.

Consider this, when was the last time a traveling exhibit of such rare and important ancient artifacts displayed at an inner city community college in middle America? Sure it would be expensive due to logistics and security, but if anyone could afford to do it, it would be the 1%. I guess even philanthropy has its limits. Then how about funding more scholarships to send these hypothetical students to where the artifacts are kept?

Perhaps my passion and specificity comes from a place of personal experience. I was an impoverished community college student once. I also helped teach disadvantaged young people archaeology, literally in the middle of an inner city housing project. History belongs to 100% of us. It is not the domain of only 1%. There needs to be a greater effort to promote interest in history among the general public. History is a dynamic and living field. Don't be confused about this fact, just because history deals with dead people and dusty artifacts. It is alive with discovery, debate, and discourse! The only people who still want us to think about history as being an exercise in the rote memorization of dates and facts are the people who place themselves in positions of authority.

As a historian, I can assure you that right now, scholars actively debate and questions almost every historical fact out there. Don't let anybody tell you that it's all figured out, now go memorize and repeat it. That is control. We must continue to fight for freethinking. We must read the authors and the theories that the mainstream shuns. We must embrace our own cultural heritage and the cultural heritage of others.

Let's create a public discourse about these, and other issues about our past so that the only history makers are us. Academics, indeed, play an important role in this. However, their role should be that of a knowledgeable guide, not an infallible dictator. The more we can teach others that history, as well as all academic pursuits, is something to do, as opposed to something to view, the more we can elevate the overall intellect of humanity. When it comes to our history, we must stop being simply watchers. We must instead, become participants.

EPILOGUE

"So these elongated skulls, would you say they are alien?"

"No. I mean, they seem strange, but the practice of artificial cranial deformation predates written history. Milder forms of intentional cranial deformation are still practiced by various groups worldwide. In fact…"

"Would you say that *other* people say they are alien?" Looking up from her clipboard, Janice, the producer, leaned back and folder her arms.

"Well, I mean, I guess. Yeah." I said. "However, the classic examples commonly referenced today, show that…"

"So other archaeologists claim these elongated skulls are definitive proof of ancient extraterrestrial contact. Is this what you are telling me?" Janice leaned in closer.

I got lost in the rhythm of her pen tapping against her acrylic nails.

"Can you just repeat that for me? Dr. Lynn?"

"Repeat what?" I asked, still hypnotized by her incessant pen clicking.

"Can you just repeat after me? Archaeologists claim…"

Slightly lowering her head, she repeated with more emphasis, "Archaeologists claim…"

"Archaeologists claim." I parroted.

"These elongated skulls are definitive proof of ancient extraterrestrial contact." continued Janice.

"These elongated skulls are definitive proof of ancient extraterrestrial contact." I bluntly repeated.

"Awesome! You look great! Your teeth are so white, aren't they Joe?" Janice said, looking to her left. A man walked out from behind the camera gave a thumbs up.

"I think her hair looks great! Our female demographic is gonna love this just as much as our male. Can we get some powder, though? Her face is shiny like she's been eating fried chicken or something." scoffed Joe through a squinted eye.

With a sparkle of adoration in her eye, Janice stood up and said, "That's a real compliment coming from Joe. He knows his stuff. He's done a lot of work shooting for Playboy and a ton of Hollywood reality shows. We only use the best talent here!"

She abruptly looked back at me and said, "Our job is to make *you* look good. Your job, is to make *us* look good. Do you have any powder or makeup?"

"Yeah, it's in the bag that your production assistant took from me." I said.

Escorting me off set, Janice said, "Awesome. Go find it and powder your nose. When you come back, I want you to repeat what you were saying about those long skulls being proof of aliens. This time, let's see if we can emphasize the words 'proof' and 'extraterrestrial.' You are rockin' this, girlfriend! Also, do you know anything about Japanese flood myths? We need a Japanese expert."

"No. I really don't."

"Can you just fake it?" she asked.

"I really wouldn't feel right faking it. I wouldn't even know what to say."

I felt at that moment that I had disappointed her. "I'm sorry. If you want to talk about Sumerian or Babylonian flood myths then I'm your girl!" I said, raising my right thumb in a feigned gesture of good humor.

"Yeah, well. We did something on that already last season. We are trying something new. Tell you what, I'll write some things for you to say. Like I said, we'll make you look good. Just do the same in return. Give us something we can use."

"Didn't you just have a professor on before me who was a Japanese history expert?" I asked, as it had occurred to me.

"Yeah but he wasn't the least bit entertaining." Janice said, rolling her eyes.

"He was very accurate, though. I heard a little of his interview." I said.

"We're in the business of entertaining, not informing. You know what I mean, right? Are we ready?" Janice asked, sounding as though she was about to start a cheer at a high school football game.

"Okay. Here is what I want you to say, Dr. Lynn. Look straight into the camera and say that archaeologists are baffled by all of the similarities between flood myths, and then if you could talk about Atlantis that would be great." Janice instructed.

"Well, I can say that archaeologists are intrigued by the similarities between flood myths, but baffled, well that's implying a lot more than I think we need to. As far as Atlantis, I can comment on Plato's Atlantis and modern theories about where it may have been located."

"Well, that's fine. Can you get into some of the Atlantian mythology and how some researchers believe that Atlantians may have been a tall, blond, and blue eyed race of people?"

Her voice seemed to fade into the distance as I started to realize that I had compromised my beliefs. I risked becoming a mouthpiece for the establishment. How can any of us free ourselves from this matrix when we are less interested in truth and more interested in glamor and entertainment?

My heart sank and I lowered my head, perhaps in shame, only to catch a glimpse of Janice's calf as she crossed her legs, exposing a purple butterfly tattoo. Symbols and associations surround us. It is easy to connect dots, but each picture we create will be unique to our perspectives.

It was then that I realized, that if I continued, I would become part of the problem. I knew what I had to do. I had to pull back from the spotlight and double down on the research. If not, I would run the risk of "selling out." To do so would make me vulnerable to future disinformation campaigns. I have witnessed so many sell out over the years. An age old NWO trick is to raise a person up to cult-like status, only to use them to march their followers off a cliff like the Pied Piper; one of their favorite allegories. At best, these "celebrities" become controlled opposition after being beckoned by the cult of personality. At worst, they are destroyed.

You will not hear me play a pipe. I will march to the beat of my own drum, as should you. Despite the ease with which the NWO is able to homogenize culture, individuality, no matter how small, is powerful enough to threaten the fragile stability of their global agenda.

END NOTES

1. Malina, Bruce J., and John J. Pilch. *Social-science Commentary on the Book of Revelation*. Minneapolis: Fortress Press, 2000.

2. Hancock, Graham, and Robert Bauval. *The Message of the Sphinx: A Quest for the Hidden Legacy of Mankind*. Broadway Books, 1997.

3. Campbell, Stuart, Robert Killick, and Jane Moon. "Ur Region Archaeology Project: 9 ICAANE Poster." 2014.

4. "URAP 2013 Report | Ur Region Archaeology Project." 2013.

5. "Tell Khaiber - Timeline Photos | Facebook." Tell Khaiber - Timeline Photos | Facebook. March 9, 2015. Accessed March 10, 2015. https://www.facebook.com/tellkhaiber/photos/a.553448948081837.1073741828.551062171653848/783956311697765/?type=1&theater.

6. Leakey, R. E. F. "Early Homo Sapiens Remains from the Omo River Region of South-west Ethiopia: Faunal Remains from the Omo Valley." *Nature*, 1969, 1132-133.

7.   Millard, A. R. (1986). "The Infancy of the Alphabet." *World Archaeology* 17 (3): 390–398. doi:10.1080/00438243.1986.9979978.

8.   In the Christian Bible, there is one mention in Genesis of a land called "Shinar," which some scholar identify with Sumer. However, this word actually stands for the "Sumer-Akkad." This is a very different meaning all together thus leaving the actual Sumerians completely out of the Bible. (see Kramer, 1964)

9. Armstrong, Karen. *Fields of Blood: Religion and the History of Violence*. Knopf, 2014.

10. Kramer, Samuel Noah. *History Begins at Sumer: Thirty-nine Firsts in Man's Recorded History*. 3rd Rev. ed. Philadelphia: University of Pennsylvania Press, 1981.

11. Kramer, Samuel Noah. *The Sumerians: Their History, Culture, and Character*. Chicago: University of Chicago Press, 1963.

12. "Online Etymology Dictionary." Online Etymology Dictionary. Accessed August 21, 2014.

13. Lynn, Heather. *Anthrotheology*. Cleveland, Ohio: Midnight Crescent Publishing, 2013. 181-192.

FULL BIBLIOGRAPHY

Alter, Robert. *The Five Books of Moses: A Translation with Commentary*. New York: W.W. Norton &, 2004.

Amiran, Ruth. *Ancient Pottery of the Holy Land: From Its Beginnings in the Neolithic Period to the End of the Iron Age*. New Brunswick, N.J.: Rutgers University Press, 1970.

Armstrong, Karen. *Fields of Blood: Religion and the History of Violence*. Knopf, 2014.

Bahn, Paul G. *The Cambridge Illustrated History of Prehistoric Art*. Cambridge, U.K.: New York :, 1998.

Bailey, Alice. *Initiation, Human and Solar*. [6th ed. New York: Lucis Pub., 1951.

Bailey, Alice. *Esoteric Psychology*. New York: Lucis Pub., 19621970.

Bailey, Alice. *A Treatise on White Magic, Or, The Way of the Disciple*. New York: Lucis Pub. ;, 1979.

Barnstone, Willis, and Marvin W. Meyer. *The Gnostic Bible*. Boston, Mass.: Shambhala, 2003.

Beaton, Kendall. "Studies in Early Petroleum History." *Business History Review* Bus. Hist. Rev. 2, no. 1 (1961): 130-31.

Blavatsky, H. P. *Isis Unveiled: A Master-key to the Mysteries of Ancient and Modern Science and Theology*. Pasadena, Calif.: Theosophical University Press, 1972.

Booth, Mark. *The Secret History of the World*. New York: Overlook Press, 2008.

Brockway, Robert W. *Myth from the Ice Age to Mickey Mouse*. Albany: State University of New York Press, 1993.

Campbell, Joseph. *The Masks of God: Primitive Mythology*. New York: Viking Press, 1959.

Cathcart, Kevin J., Carmel McCarthy, and John F. Healey. *Biblical and Near Eastern Essays*

Studies in Honour of Kevin J. Cathcart. London: T & T Clark International, 2004.

Churchward, Albert. *The Arcana of Freemasonry*. Boston: WeiserBooks, 2005.

Clark, Kenneth. *Civilisation: A Personal View*. New York: Harper & Row, 1970.

Crowley, Aleister, and Frieda Harris. The *Book of Thoth*. York Beach, Me.: S. Weiser, 1974.

Dalley, Stephanie. *Myths from Mesopamia: Creation, the Flood, Gilgamesh, and Others*. Oxford [England: Oxford University Press, 1989.

Durant, Will, and Ariel Durant. *The Age of Voltaire,*. New York: Simon and Schuster, 1965.

"ETCSLhomepage." ETCSLhomepage. Accessed April 18, 2013.

Fagan, Brian M. *Return to Babylon: Travelers, Archaeologists, and Monuments in Mesopotamia*. Boston: Little, Brown, 1979.

Frale, Barbara. *The Templars and the Shroud of Christ*. New York: Skyhorse Pub., 2012.

Greene, B. *The Fabric of the Cosmos: Space, Time, and the Texture of Reality*. New York: A.A. Knopf, 2004.

Hancock, Graham, and Robert Bauval. *The Message of the Sphinx: A Quest for the Hidden Legacy of Mankind*. Broadway Books, 1997.

Heindel, Max. *The Rosicrucian Cosmo-conception; Or, Mystic Christianity. An Elementary Treatise upon Man's past Evolution, Present Constitution and Future Development*. 26th ed. Oceanside, Calif.: Rosicrucian Fellowship;, 1971.

Jonas, Hans. *The Gnostic Religion*. 2d ed. Boston: Beacon Press, 1963.

Kleiner, Fred S., and Helen Gardner. *Gardner's Art through the Ages: A Global History*. 14th ed. Australia: Wadsworth, Cengage Learning, 2013.

Kramer, Samuel Noah. *Sumerian Mythology; a Study of Spiritual and Literary Achievement in the Third Millennium B.C.* Rev. ed. New York: Harper, 1961.

Kramer, Samuel Noah. *The Sumerians: Their History, Culture, and Character*. Chicago: University of Chicago Press, 1963.

Lando, Barry. *Web of Deceit: The History of Western Complicity in Iraq, from Churchill to Kennedy to George W. Bush*. New York: Other Press, 2007.

Layard, Austen Henry. *Nineveh and Its Remains: With an Account of a Visit to the Chaldæan Christians of Kurdistan, and the Yezidis, or Devil-worshippers, and an Inquiry into the Manners and Arts of the Ancient Assyrians*. New York: George P. Putnam, 1849.

Leakey, R. E. F. "Early Homo Sapiens Remains from the Omo River Region of South-west Ethiopia: Faunal Remains from the Omo Valley." *Nature*, 1969, 1132-133.

Lessa, William Armand, and Evon Z. Vogt. *Reader in Comparative Religion: An Anthropological Approach*. 2d ed. New York: Harper & Row, 1965.

Lynn, Heather. *Anthrotheology*. Cleveland, Ohio: Midnight Crescent Publishing, 2013.

Lynn, Heather. *The Sumerian Controversy*. Cleveland, Ohio: Midnight Crescent Publishing, 2013.

Magli, Giulio. "Sirius and the Project of the Megalithic Enclosures at ..." Cornell University Library. July 31, 2013.

Malina, Bruce J., and John J. Pilch. *Social-science Commentary on the Book of Revelation*. Minneapolis: Fortress Press, 2000.

Marcovich, Miroslav. "From Ishtar to Aphrodite." *Journal of Aesthetic Education* 30, no. 2 (1996): 43-59. 1996. Accessed August 5, 2013. http://www.jstor.org/stable/3333191.

Marrs, Jim. *Our Occulted History: Do the Global Elite Conceal Ancient Aliens?* New York: William Morrow, 2013.

Merrifield, Ralph. *The Archaeology of Ritual and Magic*. New York: New Amsterdam, 1988.

Moro, Andrea, and Noam Chomsky. *The Boundaries of Babel: The Brain and the Enigma of Impossible Languages*. Cambridge, Mass.: MIT Press, 2008.

Müller, F. Max. *Lectures on the Origin and Growth of Religion as Illustrated by the Religions of India Delivered in the Chapter House, Westminster Abbey, in April, May, and June, 1878.* New York: Scribner, 1879.

Müller, F. Max. *The Sacred Books of the East,.* Oxford: Clarendon Press, 18791910.

Noll, Richard. *The Aryan Christ: The Secret Life of Carl Jung.* New York: Random House, 1997.

Pagels, Elaine H. *The Gnostic Gospels.* New York: Random House, 1979.

Podlecki, Anthony J. *The Persians.* Englewood Cliffs, N.J.: Prentice-Hall, 1970.

Puchner, Martin. *The Norton Anthology of World Literature.* 3rd ed. New York: W.W. Norton &, 2012.

Rubenstein, Jay. *Armies of Heaven: The First Crusade and the Quest for Apocalypse.* New York: Basic Books, 2011.

Runes, Dagobert D. *Pictorial History of Philosophy.* New York: Philosophical Library, 1959.

Sagan, Carl. *Cosmos*. New York: Random House, 1980.

Sitchin, Zecharia. *The 12th Planet*. Santa Fe, N.M.: Bear &, 1991.

Sitchin, Zecharia. *There Were Giants upon the Earth: Gods, Demigods, and Human Ancestry : The Evidence of Alien DNA*. Rochester, Vt.: Bear &, 2010.

"Tell Khaiber - Timeline Photos | Facebook." Tell Khaiber - Timeline Photos | Facebook. March 9, 2015. Accessed March 10, 2015. https://www.facebook.com/tellkhaiber/photos/a.553448948081837.1073741828.5510621 71653848/783956311697765/?type=1&theater

Zolar's *Encyclopedia of Ancient and Forbidden Knowledge*. New York: Prentice Hall, 19891984.

***

ABOUT THE AUTHOR

Heather Lynn is a leading expert in alternative archaeology and hidden history. She is a professional historian, archaeologist, and member of the Association of Ancient Historians, World Archaeological Congress, and founder of the Society for Truth in Archaeological Research (STAR). Heather broke away from the mainstream after realizing that much of what we know about our history is based solely on the consensus of elite, often politically motivated, individuals and institutions. Now, she is on a quest to expose the intricate network of corrupt academic elites, global power brokers, and international banking families that work together to revise human history.

While Heather Lynn is both an academically trained historian and archaeologist, her open-minded approach is what makes her a true renegade. Heather's research includes archaeology, history, religion, mythology, Near Eastern religion, metaphysics, and spirituality. On a given day, she can be found in a library, museum, lab, or in the field investigating anomalous discoveries.

Official Website: **www.drheatherlynn.com**

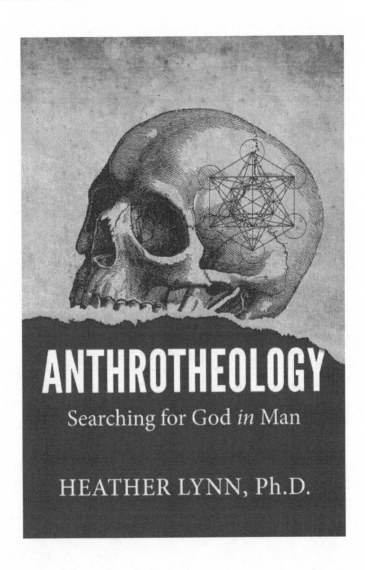

There is ancient knowledge so powerful, it has been hidden, distorted, and used to enslave humanity for thousands of years. Using an interdisciplinary approach to archaeology, combined with personal experiences and metaphysical insight, historian and archaeologist, Heather Lynn, presents questions and theories about the origin of human consciousness, God, and the power structures that have come to dominate our world.

Amid modern science, occult wisdom, metaphysics, and mythology, what do we really know about consciousness? What do we really know about ourselves? *Anthrotheology* is an empowering and thought provoking book that will change the way you look at the world, and yourself.

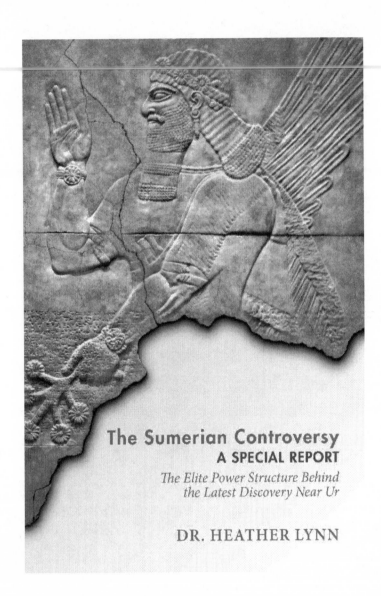

The Sumerian Controversy
A SPECIAL REPORT
*The Elite Power Structure Behind
the Latest Discovery Near Ur*

DR. HEATHER LYNN

In her bestselling report that started it all, *The Sumerian Controversy*, Dr. Heather Lynn lifts the veil and exposes the elite power structure behind the latest discovery near the ancient city of Ur (modern day Iraq).

What is the connection to big oil, bankers, and elite families? Among many of the new artifacts, one stands out that has been quickly shipped off for analysis. It speaks of royal bloodlines...

This brief report is the first part of a series of designed to keep the public informed on this unfolding story. If we work together, the truth can be brought to light.

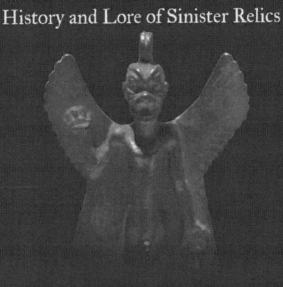

EVIL
ARCHAEOLOGY
History and Lore of Sinister Relics

HEATHER LYNN, Ph.D.

Demons, jinn, possession, sinister artifacts, and gruesome archaeological discoveries haunt the pages of the new book by Dr. Heather Lynn. Evil Archaeology investigates the archaeological record for artifacts and evidence of evil entities. It also looks at the history and lore behind real relics, believed to be haunted.

Is there really a prehistoric fertility goddess figure that has been known to bring death to the families of anyone who holds it? Are there real vampire graveyards? Can the archaeological record prove the existence of demons and malevolent entities? Evil Archaeology contains interviews and accounts from real-life exorcists and is not for the easily frightened.

Made in the USA
San Bernardino, CA
18 February 2018